Contents

1. Family Conflict Among Chinese- and Mexican-Origin Adolescents and Their Parents in the U.S.: An Introduction 1
Linda P. Juang, Adriana J. Umaña-Taylor
The authors set the stage for the rest of the volume by discussing developmental and cultural sources of parent–adolescent conflict and highlight how the chapters in the volume address key contexts and processes related to family conflict and adolescent adjustment.

2. Acculturation-Based and Everyday Family Conflict in Chinese American Families 13
Linda P. Juang, Moin Syed, Jeffrey T. Cookston, Yijie Wang, Su Yeong Kim
The authors integrate our knowledge of these two types of family conflict that have been studied separately to arrive at a new understanding of what family conflict means for Chinese American adolescents and their parents.

3. Conflicts and Communication Between High-Achieving Chinese American Adolescents and Their Parents 35
Desiree Baolian Qin, Tzu-Fen Chang, Eun-Jin Han, Grace Chee
Based on in-depth interview data, the authors explore various domains of conflict that high-achieving Chinese American youth and their parents engage in, the process by which these conflicts emerge, and youths' perceptions of how conflicts are resolved.

4. Mother–Daughter Conflict and Adjustment in Mexican-Origin Families: Exploring the Role of Family and Sociocultural Context 59
Kimberly A. Updegraff, Adriana J. Umaña-Taylor, Norma J. Perez-Brena, Jacqueline Pflieger
Drawing from ecologically oriented and person–environment fit models, the authors investigate how the family context, as defined by the transition to adolescent motherhood, and the sociocultural context, as measured by mother–daughter discrepancies in cultural orientations, shape the associations between conflict and adjustment in Mexican-origin families.

5. Guided Cognitive Reframing of Adolescent–Father Conflict: Who Mexican American and European American Adolescents Seek and Why 83
Jeffrey T. Cookston, Andres F. Olide, Michele A. Adams, William V. Fabricius, Ross D. Parke
The authors offer a conceptual model of guided cognitive reframing that emphasizes the behavioral, cognitive, and affective implications of

confidant support as well as individual, family, and cultural factors linked to support seeking among Mexican- and European-heritage adolescents.

6. Gaps, Conflicts, and Arguments Between Adolescents and Their Parents 105
Andrew J. Fuligni
In this commentary, the author highlights the unique contributions of each chapter and suggests that distinguishing between three types of parent–adolescent differences—acculturation gaps, feelings of conflict, and actual arguments between adolescents and their parents—provides a way to understand the findings on immigrant family conflict presented in this volume.

INDEX 111

New Directions for Child and Adolescent Development

Lene Arnett Jensen
Reed W. Larson
EDITORS-IN-CHIEF

William Damon
FOUNDING EDITOR

Family Conflict Among Chinese- and Mexican-Origin Adolescents and Their Parents in the U.S.

Linda P. Juang
Adriana J. Umaña-Taylor
EDITORS

Number 135 • Spring 2012
Jossey-Bass
San Francisco

FAMILY CONFLICT AMONG CHINESE- AND MEXICAN-ORIGIN ADOLESCENTS
AND THEIR PARENTS IN THE U.S.
Linda P. Juang, Adriana J. Umaña-Taylor (eds.)
New Directions for Child and Adolescent Development, no. 135
Lene Arnett Jensen, Reed W. Larson, Editors-in-Chief

© 2012 Wiley Periodicals, Inc., A Wiley Company. All rights reserved.

No part of this publication may be reproduced, stored in a retrieval system, or transmitted in any form or by any means, electronic, mechanical, photocopying, recording, scanning, or otherwise, except as permitted under Sections 107 or 108 of the 1976 United States Copyright Act, without either the prior written permission of the Publisher or authorization through payment of the appropriate per-copy fee to the Copyright Clearance Center, 222 Rosewood Drive, Danvers, MA 01923; (978) 750-8400, fax (978) 646-8600. Requests to the Publisher for permission should be addressed to the Permissions Department, John Wiley & Sons, Inc., 111 River St., Hoboken, NJ 07030, (201) 748-6011, fax (201) 748-6008, www.wiley.com/go/permissions.

Microfilm copies of issues and articles are available in 16mm and 35mm, as well as microfiche in 105mm, through University Microfilms, Inc., 300 North Zeeb Road, Ann Arbor, Michigan 48106-1346.

ISSN 1520-3247   electronic ISSN 1534-8687

NEW DIRECTIONS FOR CHILD AND ADOLESCENT DEVELOPMENT is part of The Jossey-Bass Education Series and is published quarterly by Wiley Subscription Services, Inc., a Wiley company, at Jossey-Bass, One Montgomery Street, Suite 1200, San Francisco, CA 94104-4594. Periodicals postage paid at San Francisco, California, and at additional mailing offices. Postmaster: Send address changes to New Directions for Child and Adolescent Development, Jossey-Bass, One Montgomery Street, Suite 1200, San Francisco, CA 94104-4594.

New Directions for Child and Adolescent Development is indexed in Cambridge Scientific Abstracts (CSA/CIG), CHID: Combined Health Information Database (NIH), Contents Pages in Education (T&F), Current Abstracts (EBSCO), Educational Research Abstracts Online (T&F), EMBASE/Excerpta Medica (Elsevier), ERIC Database (Education Resources Information Center), Index Medicus/MEDLINE/PubMed (NLM), Linguistics & Language Behavior Abstracts (CSA/CIG), Psychological Abstracts/PsycINFO (APA), Social Services Abstracts (CSA/CIG), SocINDEX (EBSCO), and Sociological Abstracts (CSA/CIG).

SUBSCRIPTION rates: For the U.S., $89 for individuals and $343 for institutions. Please see ordering information page at end of journal.

EDITORIAL CORRESPONDENCE should be e-mailed to the editors-in-chief: Lene Arnett Jensen (ljensen@clarku.edu) and Reed W. Larson (larsonr@illinois.edu).

Jossey-Bass Web address: www.josseybass.com

Juang, L. P., & Umaña-Taylor, A. J. (2012). Family conflict among Chinese- and Mexican-origin adolescents and their parents in the U.S.: An introduction. In L. P. Juang & A. J. Umaña-Taylor (Eds.), *Family conflict among Chinese- and Mexican-origin adolescents and their parents in the U.S. New Directions for Child and Adolescent Development*, 135, 1–12.

1

Family Conflict Among Chinese- and Mexican-Origin Adolescents and Their Parents in the U.S.: An Introduction

Linda P. Juang, Adriana J. Umaña-Taylor

Abstract

This volume explores how cultural and family contexts inform parent–adolescent conflict and adjustment among Chinese- and Mexican-origin families in the United States. Collectively, the chapters examine outcomes associated with family conflict and provide an in-depth analysis of how and for whom conflict is related to adjustment. Findings, for example, illustrate how cultural factors (e.g., acculturation) modify the links between conflict and adjustment. Furthermore, the collection allows for a simultaneous examination of normative, everyday parent–adolescent conflict and conflict that is specific to the process of cultural adaptation, and furthers our understanding of how both developmental and cultural sources of conflict are linked to adjustment. © 2012 Wiley Periodicals, Inc.

All families fight—some more than others. From a developmental perspective, conflict with parents during adolescence (at least at moderate levels) is a healthy part of youth development (Laursen, Coy, & Collins, 1998) and serves several important and interrelated developmental functions. One important function is to promote autonomy during adolescence (Fuligni, 1998; Smetana, 2002; Steinberg & Morris, 2001). As adolescents become older, they are expected to manage their daily activities (e.g., behavioral autonomy; Feldman & Rosenthal, 1991), as well as take part in families' decision-making process (Smetana, Campione-Barr, & Daddis, 2004). Another function of parent–adolescent conflict is to provide opportunities to revise and transform parent–adolescent expectations, roles, and responsibilities so that parent–adolescent relationships remain developmentally appropriate (Laursen et al., 1998; Youniss & Smollar, 1985). Finally, conflict is important for establishing and defining a value and belief system, contributing to adolescent identity development as adolescents reflect, evaluate, and construct who they are and what they believe in (Bruner, 1990). Taken together, parent–adolescent conflict serves to promote adolescent development in key areas such as autonomy, relationships, and identity.

However, viewing conflict as healthy and developmentally adaptive has been traditionally limited to conclusions drawn from empirical studies focused primarily on European American families (Laursen et al., 1998; Smetana, 1988). In these studies, the emphasis has been on normative conflict over "minor" everyday issues (Laursen et al., 1998; Smetana, 1988). In contrast, studies of parent–adolescent conflict involving immigrant families of Asian and Latino heritage have primarily focused on disruptive conflict over more "serious" issues concerning core cultural values, namely, acculturation-based conflict (Portes & Rumbaut, 1996, 2001; Rivera et al., 2008). Less is known about whether acculturation-based conflict is normative and whether it is a healthy part of youth development. Indeed, Smetana (2008) has recently highlighted the need for more studies on conflict in ethnically and culturally diverse families. Specifically, there is a need for studies that identify culturally relevant characteristics contributing to parent–adolescent interactions and relationships, and subsequent adolescent outcomes.

To address this need, the current volume explores family conflict among Chinese and Mexican heritage adolescents and their parents, as these two national origin groups, respectively, represent the largest subgroups within the panethnic Asian and Latino populations in the United States (U.S. Census, 2010, 2011). We address questions such as, Are everyday and acculturation-based conflicts similarly linked to youth adjustment, and do they follow similar pathways in their links to adjustment? How are conflicts resolved? Are the negative effects of family conflict exacerbated by parent–adolescent acculturation discrepancies and other aspects of the family context? And to whom do adolescents turn to make meaning of the conflict in which they are engaged? Given the limited research in this area with these populations, we know little about within-group variability that may exist in youth and families' experiences with parent–adolescent conflict. Our goal for this volume is to not only examine the "outcomes" associated with family conflict but to also provide an in-depth analysis of the contexts and processes that explain *how* family conflict is related to adjustment and for whom. The current volume provides a unique opportunity to showcase the complexity of parent–adolescent conflict among Chinese- and Mexican-origin families in the United States and makes an important contribution to a literature in which there is limited knowledge on normative developmental process among ethnic minority populations (García Coll et al., 1996; McLoyd, 1998).

A Focus on Chinese- and Mexican-Origin Families in the U.S.

In the last two decades, almost 80% of immigrants to the United States have originated from Asia and Latin America (Passel, 2011). Today, individuals of Chinese and Mexican origin represent the two largest national origin groups within the panethnic Asian (23%) and Latino (66%) populations in the United States, respectively (U.S. Census Bureau, 2008). These two groups experienced tremendous population growth because of continued migration to the United States. In addition, they experienced such high fertility rates that between the years 1960 and 2006 the foreign-born population from China increased by 300%, and between 1980 and 2008 the foreign-born population from Mexico increased by 100% (Migration Policy Institute, 2010a, 2010b).

Beyond the shared distinction of being among the most rapidly growing subpopulations in the United States, the two groups share other important characteristics: Both represent numeric ethnic minorities in the United States, and both include large numbers of immigrant families. To understand the development of Chinese- and Mexican-heritage adolescents, three factors must be considered: issues pertinent to normative adolescent development, issues pertinent to ethnic minority status, and issues pertinent to the immigration experience (Phinney, Ong, & Madden, 2000). García Coll and colleagues' (1996) integrative developmental model of minority children is a useful theoretical framework that carefully considers all three factors.

García Coll and colleagues (1996) argue that beyond normative developmental issues relevant for all adolescents (e.g., biological and cognitive changes associated with different developmental ages), explicit attention must be paid to the role of social position variables (e.g., gender, socioeconomic status [SES], ethnic minority status). Social position variables such as ethnic minority status indirectly contribute to child development by exposing children to powerful social mechanisms (such as discrimination and prejudice) as they attempt to navigate their way through the majority culture. These negative experiences within social hierarchies can be challenging and may adversely impact family relationships by contributing stress to family interactions. Such experiences can be critical influences in children's development.

In addition to issues related to ethnic minority status, immigration-related issues must also be considered. Notably, about 85% of Asian-heritage children and 60% of Latino-heritage children are of immigrant background (i.e., have at least one parent who was born outside of the United States; Passel, 2011). These numbers underscore the need to consider processes related to migration such as acculturation. As an example, because Chinese- and Mexican-heritage parents and adolescents are negotiating two cultural systems, and because children tend to acquire the values and behaviors of the mainstream culture faster and more thoroughly than their parents do, a discrepancy in values and behaviors may result. This parent–child acculturation discrepancy has been termed the *acculturation gap* (Kwak, 2003), *acculturation dissonance* (Portes & Rumbaut, 1996), and *acculturative family distancing* (Hwang, Wood, & Fujimoto, 2010). Acculturation researchers have hypothesized that the greater the acculturation gap, the greater the potential for parent–child conflict, and subsequently child maladjustment (Portes & Rumbaut, 1996). A common assumption of immigrant families (for which there is some evidence) is that because they must balance two different, sometimes opposing, cultures, they are at risk for greater family conflict (Kwak, 2003; Portes & Rumbaut, 1996, 2001). However, a recent review of the acculturation gap literature suggests that the relation between acculturation gaps, family conflict, and adolescent adjustment is much more complex than is usually presented (Telzer, 2011). Importantly, Telzer's (2011) review suggests that the acculturation process and resulting acculturation discrepancies do not inevitably occur and, when they do occur, they do not inevitably lead to greater family conflict. In this volume, we consider family conflict in relation to characteristics of the adolescent, family context, and broader sociocultural context, to demonstrate that the consequences of family conflict depend on all of these variables, and not simply on the absolute difference between a parent's level of acculturation and an adolescent's.

What Can We Learn from Studying Parent–Adolescent Conflict in Chinese- and Mexican-Origin Families?

To understand conflict within Chinese- and Mexican-origin families, it is important to consider the aspects of family conflict that are salient for all adolescents, the aspects that are salient only for adolescents of a particular cultural/ethnic background, and the aspects that may be unique based on particular family or individual characteristics. Some aspects of family conflict appear to be relevant to both Chinese- and Mexican-origin families and all families in general. There is evidence that the level, function, and consequences of parent–adolescent conflict show similarities across various ethnicities and cultural backgrounds. For instance, in general, using varied methodologies such as surveys and daily diaries, studies have shown that the frequency of everyday conflict is rather low or moderate for families of Chinese and Mexican heritage (Chung, Flook, & Fuligni, 2009; Fuligni, 1998; Yau & Smetana, 2003). Further, engaging in low or moderate parent–adolescent conflict is normative for families of diverse cultural backgrounds, with the important role of promoting autonomy during adolescence (Fuligni, 1998; Smetana, 2002; Steinberg & Morris, 2001). Studies have also established that greater parent–adolescent conflict is associated with negative adolescent adjustment, such as greater emotional distress, at least in the short-term, for both Chinese-origin (Juang, Syed, & Takagi, 2007; Kim, Chen, Li, Huang, & Moon, 2009; Qin, 2006) and Mexican-origin adolescents (Lau et al., 2005; Pasch et al., 2006; Updegraff, Delgado, & Wheeler, 2009). Because parents of all cultures share the developmental goals of promoting autonomy and maintaining connectedness with their children (Tamis-LeMonda et al., 2008), and adolescents of various cultures increasingly believe that certain domains of their lives should be under their own personal authority (Smetana, 2002), similarities in parent–adolescent conflict should be expected in families across diverse groups. Therefore, by studying both Chinese- and Mexican-heritage families, we can uncover what aspects of parent–adolescent conflict may be similar and applicable across ethnic groups, and what aspects may be unique to each group.

Chinese- and Mexican-origin families share an important characteristic—both groups are defined by a relatively strong cultural emphasis on family obligation, interdependence, harmony, and conformity to parental expectations (i.e., filial piety and familism). Indeed, a recent study found that individuals of Asian- and Latino-background reported similar levels of filial piety and familism and that both groups reported higher levels compared with European American individuals (Schwartz et al., 2010). Given the similarities between Chinese and Mexican cultures with respect to the emphasis on the family, it is possible that we could extrapolate what we find with Chinese-heritage families to what we find with Mexican-heritage families and vice versa. Indeed, the common thread that runs through the chapters in this volume is the focus on understanding how features of the cultural and family contexts give meaning to the experiences of parent–adolescent conflict in Chinese- and Mexican-origin families. Specifically, Juang and colleagues (Juang, Syed, Cookston, Wang, & Kim, this volume) examine the role of parenting and family cohesion in the associations between parent–adolescent conflict and Chinese American youth adjustment; Updegraff and colleagues (Updegraff, Umaña-Taylor, Perez-Brena, & Pflieger, this volume) and Cookston and colleagues (Cookston, Olide, Adams, Fabricius, & Parke, this volume) examine how features of the family context introduce variability into parent–adolescent conflict and its link to Mexican-origin youth adjustment; finally, Qin and colleagues (Qin, Chang, Han, & Chee, this volume) consider how cultural norms regarding parent–child relationships may shape parent–adolescent conflict in Chinese American families. Given the strong emphasis on family in both of these cultural groups, understanding these complex associations in one ethnic sample may shed light on the mechanisms that are at play in the other, and vice versa.

There are, of course, variations within the broad ethnic groups of Chinese- and Mexican-heritage families. For instance, both Updegraff et al. and Cookston et al. (this volume) explore how variations in the family context (i.e., mother–adolescent relationship within the context of teenage pregnancy; two-parent versus single-parent family constellation) have implications for adolescent well-being and whom adolescents turn to when sharing stories of engaging in conflict with their parent. By systematically exploring the diversity inherent within each group, we move away from the simplistic and inaccurate view that families categorized under the same ethnic label are uniformly alike. Further, measuring culturally relevant characteristics, such as cultural orientation to heritage and traditional culture, allows researchers to study ethnicity as a dynamic and developmental variable—attitudes, values, behaviors, and beliefs can change over time, but ethnic group categories do not.

How Do the Chapters in this Volume Collectively Move the Field Forward?

Two chapters in this volume address parent–adolescent conflict within Chinese-heritage families and two chapters address parent–adolescent conflict within Mexican-heritage families. Juang and colleagues examine how everyday conflict and acculturation-based conflict uniquely relate to Chinese American adolescent development. The chapter draws upon two longitudinal survey-based data sets to illustrate the importance of understanding both types of conflict for Chinese American adolescent adjustment. Qin and colleagues focus on family conflict and communication between high-achieving Chinese American adolescents and their parents. In contrast to the previous chapter, Qin and colleagues' chapter adopts a qualitative approach to provide an in-depth exploration of various domains of conflict that high achieving youth and their parents engage in, the process by which these conflicts emerge, and youths' perceptions of how conflicts are resolved. The next two chapters focus on Mexican-origin families and consider adolescent conflict with mothers and fathers separately. Updegraff and colleagues explore how Mexican-origin mother–daughter conflict varies by family context (e.g., families with pregnant adolescent daughters vs. families with nonpregnant adolescent daughters). This chapter draws upon two datasets of Mexican-origin mothers and daughters and adopts an ecological approach by assessing family conflict within contrasting family contexts and the broader sociocultural context. Cookston and colleagues, in contrast, focus on Mexican-origin adolescents' conflict with fathers. Their findings illustrate how adolescents deal with conflict with fathers by turning to confidants, and subsequently how they make sense of the conflict after talking with confidants. This chapter, like the previous, also pays attention to varying family contexts (by comparing adolescents with a biological father vs. stepfather). A recurring theme in each of the four chapters is consideration of family conflict within the context of the acculturation process for both parents and adolescents. The final chapter in the volume is a commentary provided by Andrew J. Fuligni who has worked extensively with immigrant adolescents and families. His commentary emphasizes the need for a more nuanced and in-depth examination of the different aspects of family conflict that were covered in the four chapters (i.e., acculturation gaps, conflictual feelings, and actual arguments) in an effort to differentiate them from one another, allowing for a better understanding of the links between family conflict and adjustment among adolescents of Asian and Latino backgrounds.

Collectively, the chapters and commentary in this volume move the field forward in several ways. First, the contributions in this volume illustrate how cultural characteristics and experiences (e.g., acculturation, enculturation, cultural values, communication patterns) modify the links between family conflict and adolescent adjustment, and how culturally related factors contribute to the experiences of family conflict in general. Second, the collection provides an opportunity to simultaneously consider normative, everyday parent–adolescent conflict and conflict that is specific to the process of cultural adaptation. A side-by-side examination of these two aspects of family conflict moves the field forward by considering the unique contributions that each of these types of conflict makes to the family experiences of Chinese- and Mexican-origin youth. Finally, the volume includes studies that describe diverse methods (i.e., qualitative and quantitative), and between the four empirical chapters, draws upon six datasets that were collected in California, New York, and Arizona. These three states have among the largest proportion of youth who are of immigrant background (California 49%, New York 34%, and Arizona 32%; Passel, 2011).

In sum, although parent–adolescent conflict in immigrant families has long been conceptualized as inevitable due to the inherent stresses of the acculturation process, the chapters in this volume expand that view. The four empirical chapters illustrate the central role of acculturation for understanding conflict in immigrant families, identify variables that modify the consequences of parent–adolescent conflict on adolescent adjustment, and identify mediating factors that explain the link between parent–adolescent conflict and adolescent adjustment. Importantly, the chapters provide a more complex view of the interplay between parent–adolescent conflict and acculturation within immigrant families beyond the acculturation gap-adjustment hypothesis.

Questions Left Unanswered: Directions for Future Research

Although this volume provides in-depth accounts of correlates, processes, and contexts related to family conflict and adolescent adjustment, there are still many questions left unanswered and important issues to consider. As such, there are many avenues for future research. To date, there are few long-term longitudinal studies examining parent–adolescent conflict in immigrant families. What are, for instance, implications for engaging in conflict at age 12–13 versus at 17–18? For example, among Chinese-heritage adolescents, parent–adolescent conflict may peak during later adolescence, rather than early adolescence as is the case for European American adolescents, given that the push for autonomy among Chinese-heritage youth occurs at later ages compared with European American adolescents (Fuligni, Tseng, & Lam, 1999; Greenberger & Chen, 1996). To our knowledge, there are no longitudinal studies documenting the stability and change in parent–adolescent conflict through the course of adolescence for ethnic minority youth. Longitudinal studies are necessary to also examine possible differences in trajectories, correlates, and consequences of family conflict in relation to gender or nativity—two key variables that have not received adequate attention in studies of immigrant youth (Fuligni, 2001; Suarez-Orozco & Qin, 2006). Future studies could consider generational status in depth, perhaps by comparing third-generation families (both adolescents and parents born in the United States) with first- or second-generation families to explicitly test what features of parent–adolescent conflict are attributed directly to the migration process. It also will be important to understand whether acculturation-based conflict becomes irrelevant by the third and later generations, or whether there are unique aspects of acculturation-based conflict that persist across generations.

As noted in the beginning of this chapter, Smetana (2008) made the call to search for relevant cultural characteristics that may have implications for family conflict. Future research could explore, for instance, whether adolescents' and parents' cultural notions of shame, loss of face, or *respeto* may be consequential to family conflict. It will also be informative to move beyond examining cultural values in isolation, and consider them in concert with immediate contextual demands. García Coll and colleagues' (1996) notion of the *adaptive culture*, defined as "the product of the group's collective history (cultural, political, and economic) and the current contextual demands posed by the promoting and inhibiting environments" (p. 1904), suggests that cultural values interact with the immediate context (e.g., neighborhood safety, neighborhood resources, and support), to create another distinct context with implications for family processes. Inspired by the notion of adaptive culture, Lau's (2010) recent study of Chinese American parents found that parents who endorsed greater parental control (a key cultural value) also used more physical discipline, but only for those who also reported engaging in greater acculturation conflicts with their children (a current contextual demand). Thus, parental cultural values intersected with contextual demands to influence parenting, which may then have implications for family interactions such as family conflict. These complexities require further examination (and with multiple ethnic groups) to determine whether these are universal experiences for ethnic minority youth and families.

Finally, the chapters in the current volume contribute significantly to the literature in a number of ways, but a significant omission is a focus on understanding how parent–adolescent conflict can serve a positive function for ethnic minority youth. García Coll and Magnuson (1997) highlighted over a decade ago the need for theories to incorporate a developmental and positive orientation to immigrant children and adolescent development. For example, it will be important for future studies to explore how conflict may be constructive in immigrant families by providing opportunities to revise and transform parent–adolescent expectations, roles, and responsibilities, which is a necessary part of growing up (Laursen et al., 1998). Hopefully, this volume will contribute to the discourse on parent–adolescent conflict so that it is not viewed as an inevitable, negative, and defining characteristic of immigrant families undergoing acculturation, but rather a normative process that occurs for all families with the understanding that the broader sociohistorical contexts of immigration and ethnic minority status, coupled with each individual's unique family context, inform this important process.

References

Bruner, J. (1990). *Acts of meaning*. Cambridge, MA: Harvard University Press.

Chung, G. H., Flook, L., & Fuligni, A. J. (2009). Daily family conflict and emotional distress among adolescents from Latin American, Asian, and European backgrounds. *Developmental Psychology, 45*(5), 1406–1415. doi: 10.1037/a0014163

Feldman, S. S., & Rosenthal, D. A. (1991). Age expectations of behavioral autonomy in Hong Kong, Australian and American youth: The influence of family variables and adolescents' values. *International Journal of Psychology, 26*, 1–23.

Fuligni, A. J. (1998). Authority, autonomy, and parent–adolescent conflict and cohesion: A study of adolescents from Mexican, Chinese, Filipino, and European backgrounds. *Developmental Psychology, 34*(4), 782–792. doi: 10.1037/0012-1649.34.4.782

Fuligni, A. J. (2001). A comparative longitudinal approach to acculturation among children from immigrant families. *Harvard Educational Review, 71*(3), 566–578.

Fuligni, A. J., Tseng, V., & Lam, M. (1999). Attitudes toward family obligations among American adolescents with Asian, Latin American, and European backgrounds. *Child Development, 70*(4), 1030–1044. doi: 10.1111/1467-8624.00075

García Coll, C., Crnic, K., Lamberty, G., Wasik, B. H., Jenkins, R., Garcia, H. V., & McAdoo, H. P. (1996). An integrative model for the study of developmental competencies in minority children. *Child Development, 67*, 1891–1914.

García Coll, C., & Magnuson, K. (1997). The psychological experience of immigration: A developmental perspective. In A. Booth, A. C. Crouter, & N. S. Landale (Eds.), *Immigration and the family: Research and policy on U.S. immigrants* (pp. 91–131). Hillsdale, NJ: Erlbaum.

Greenberger, E., & Chen, C. (1996). Perceived family relationships and depressed mood in early and late adolescence: A comparison of European and Asian Americans. *Developmental Psychology, 32*(4), 707–716. doi: 10.1037/0012-1649.32.4.707

Hwang, W.-C., Wood, J. J., & Fujimoto, K. (2010). Acculturative family distancing (AFD) and depression in Chinese American families. *Journal of Consulting and Clinical Psychology, 78*(5), 655–667. doi: 10.1037/a0020542

Juang, L. P., Syed, M., & Takagi, M. (2007). Intergenerational discrepancies of parental control among Chinese American families: Links to family conflict and adolescent depressive symptoms. *Journal of Adolescence, 30*(6), 965–975. doi: 10.1016/j.adolescence.2007.01.004

Kim, S. Y., Chen, Q., Li, J., Huang, X., & Moon, U. J. (2009). Parent–child acculturation, parenting, and adolescent depressive symptoms in Chinese immigrant families. *Journal of Family Psychology, 23*(3), 426–437. doi: 10.1037/a0016019

Kwak, K. (2003). Adolescents and their parents: A review of intergenerational family relations for immigrant and non-immigrant families. *Human Development, 46*(2–3), 115–136. doi: 10.1159/000068581

Lau, A. S. (2010). Physical discipline in Chinese American immigrant families: An adaptive culture perspective. *Cultural Diversity and Ethnic Minority Psychology, 16*(3), 313–322. doi: 10.1037/a0018667

Lau, A. S., McCabe, K. M., Yeh, M., Garland, A. F., Wood, P. A., & Hough, R. L. (2005). The acculturation gap-distress hypothesis among high-risk Mexican American families. *Journal of Family Psychology, 19*(3), 367–375. doi: 10.1037/0893-3200.19.3.367

Laursen, B., Coy, K. C., & Collins, W. A. (1998). Reconsidering changes in parent–child conflict across adolescence: A meta-analysis. *Child Development, 69*(3), 817–832. doi: 10.2307/1132206

McLoyd, V. C. (1998). Changing demographics in the American population: Implications for research on minority children and adolescents. In V. C. McLoyd & L. Steinberg (Eds.), *Studying minority adolescents: Conceptual, methodological, and theoretical issues.* (pp. 3–28). Mahwah, NJ: Erlbaum.

Migration Policy Institute (2010a). U.S. in focus: Chinese immigrants in the United States. http://www.migrationinformation.org/usfocus/display.cfm?ID=781

Migration Policy Institute (2010b). U.S. in focus: Mexican immigrants in the United States. http://www.migrationinformation.org/usfocus/display.cfm?ID=767

Pasch, L. A., Deardorff, J., Tschann, J. M., Flores, E., Penilla, C., & Pantoja, P. (2006). Acculturation, parent-adolescent conflict, and adolescent adjustment in Mexican American families. *Family Process, 45*(1), 75–86. doi: 10.1111/j.1545-5300.2006.00081.x

Passel, J. S. (2011). Demography of immigrant youth: Past, present, and future. *The Future of Children, 21*(1), 19–41.

Phinney, J. S., Ong, A., & Madden, T. (2000). Cultural values and intergenerational value discrepancies in immigrant and non-immigrant families. *Child Development, 71*(2), 528–539. doi: 10.1111/1467-8624.00162

Portes, A., & Rumbaut, R. (1996). *Immigrant America: A portrait.* Berkeley, CA: University of California Press.

Portes, A., & Rumbaut, R. (2001). *Legacies: The story of the immigrant second generation.* Berkeley, CA: University of California Press.

Qin, D. B. (2006). "Our child doesn't talk to us anymore": Alienation in immigrant Chinese families. *Anthropology & Education Quarterly, 37*(2), 162–179. doi: 10.1525/aeq.2006.37.2.162

Rivera, F. I., Guarnaccia, P. J., Mulvaney-Day, N., Lin, J. Y., Torres, M., & Alegría, M. (2008). Family cohesion and its relationship to psychological distress among Latino groups. *Hispanic Journal of Behavioral Sciences, 30*(3), 357–378. doi: 10.1177/0739986308318713

Schwartz, S. J., Weisskirch, R. S., Hurley, E. A., Zamboanga, B. L., Park, I. J. K., Kim, S. Y., . . . Greene, A. D. (2010). Communalism, familism, and filial piety: Are they birds of a collectivist feather? *Cultural Diversity and Ethnic Minority Psychology, 16*(4), 548–560. doi: 10.1037/a0021370

Smetana, J. G. (1988). Concepts of self and social convention: Adolescents' and parents' reasoning about hypothetical and actual family conflicts. In M. R. Gunnar & W. A. Collins (Eds.), *Development during the transition to adolescence* (pp. 79–122). Hillsdale, NJ: Erlbaum.

Smetana, J. G. (2002). Culture, autonomy, and personal jurisdiction in adolescent-parent relationships. In R. V. Kail & H. W. Reese (Eds.), *Advances in child development and behavior* (Vol. 29, pp. 51–87). San Diego, CA: Academic Press.

Smetana, J. G. (2008). Conflicting views of conflict. *Monographs of the Society for Research in Child Development, 73*(2), 161–168. doi: 10.1111/j.1540-5834.2008.00477.x

Smetana, J. G., Campione-Barr, N., & Daddis, C. (2004). Longitudinal development of family decision making: Defining healthy behavioral autonomy for middle-class African American adolescents. *Child Development, 75*(5), 1418–1434. doi: 10.1111/j.1467-8624.2004.00749.x

Steinberg, L., & Morris, A. S. (2001). Adolescent development. *Annual Review of Psychology, 52*, 83–110. doi: 10.1146/annurev.psych.52.1.83

Suarez-Orozco, C., & Qin, D. B. (2006). Gendered perspectives in psychology: Immigrant origin youth. *International Migration Review, 40*(1), 165–198. doi: 10.1111/j.1747-7379.2006.00007.x

Tamis-LeMonda, C. S., Way, N., Hughes, D., Yoshikawa, H., Kalman, R. K., & Niwa, E. Y. (2008). Parents' goals for children: The dynamic coexistence of individualism and collectivism in cultures and individuals. *Social Development, 17*(1), 183–209.

Telzer, E. H. (2011). Expanding the acculturation gap-distress model: An integrative review of research. *Human Development, 53*(6), 313–340. doi: 10.1159/000322476

Updegraff, K. A., Delgado, M. Y., & Wheeler, L. A. (2009). Exploring mothers' and fathers' relationships with sons versus daughters: Links to adolescent adjustment in Mexican immigrant families. *Sex Roles, 60*(7–8), 559–574. doi: 10.1007/s11199-008-9527-y

U.S. Census Bureau (2008). News release: U.S. Hispanic population surpasses 45 million now 15 percent of total. Released May 1, 2008. http://www.census.gov/newsroom/releases/archives/population/cb08-67.html

U.S. Census Bureau (2010). Facts for features. Asian/Pacific American Heritage Month: May 2010.

U.S. Census Bureau (2011). The Hispanic population: 2010. 2010 Census Briefs.

Yau, J., & Smetana, J. (2003). Adolescent-parent conflict in Hong Kong and Shenzhen: A comparison of youth in two cultural contexts. *International Journal of Behavioral Development, 27*(3), 201–211. doi: 10.1080/01650250244000209

Youniss, J., & Smollar, J. (1985). *Adolescent relations with mothers, fathers, and friends*. Chicago, IL: University of Chicago Press.

LINDA P. JUANG *is a lecturer in the Department of Psychological and Brain Sciences at the University of California at Santa Barbara. E-mail: juang@psych .ucsb.edu, webpage: http://www.psych.ucsb.edu/people/faculty/juang/index.php*

ADRIANA J. UMAÑA-TAYLOR *is an associate professor in the School of Social and Family Dynamics at Arizona State University, Tempe, AZ. E-mail: Adriana .Umana-Taylor@asu.edu*

> Juang, L. P., Syed, M., Cookston, J. T., Wang, Y., & Kim, S. Y. (2012). Acculturation-based and everyday family conflict in Chinese American Families. In L. P. Juang & A. J. Umaña-Taylor (Eds.), *Family conflict among Chinese- and Mexican-origin adolescents and their parents in the U.S. New Directions for Child and Adolescent Development, 135*, 13–34.

2

Acculturation-Based and Everyday Family Conflict in Chinese American Families

Linda P. Juang, Moin Syed, Jeffrey T. Cookston, Yijie Wang, Su Yeong Kim

Abstract

Everyday conflict (studied primarily among European American families) is viewed as an assertion of autonomy from parents that is normative during adolescence. Acculturation-based conflict (studied primarily among Asian- and Latino-heritage families) is viewed as a threat to relatedness with parents rather than the normative assertion of autonomy. Our overarching goal for the chapter is to integrate our knowledge of these two types of family conflict that have been studied separately to arrive at a new understanding of what family conflict means for Chinese American adolescents and their parents. © 2012 Wiley Periodicals, Inc.

We wish to acknowledge Grant 1R24MH061573-01A1 from the National Institute of Health for funding to support Linda P. Juang's research project, Grant 5R03HD051629-02 from the National Institute of Child Health and Human Development awarded to Su Yeong Kim for funding to support her research project, the families who participated in the studies, and the research assistants who assisted with the projects. We also thank Rich Lee and the Race, Ethnicity, Migration, and Mental Health Lab for comments on an earlier draft of this chapter.

One way to conceptualize the roles of family and culture for child development is to flip the *graphic* version of Bronfenbrenner's (1979) ecological systems model inside out—so that the individual is not within the innermost circle and culture a distant outer, but where culture is in the center, radiating out to affect all the microsystems, including the family (Goodnow, 2011). Doing so would be consistent with Bronfenbrenner's *written* description of his theory, where culture takes a central position in understanding child development within the context of the family. This visual reconceptualization would help highlight how the *proximal processes* (e.g., parenting) that Bronfenbrenner hypothesized were so important for human development are themselves cultural in nature (see Figure 2.1). We adopt this perspective in the current chapter as we consider how developmental goals, rooted in a particular cultural

Figure 2.1. Conceptual model of culture in relation to self, family, and broader value system, based on Bronfenbrenner's (1979) ecological systems diagram, but with culture depicted at the core instead of the outer circle

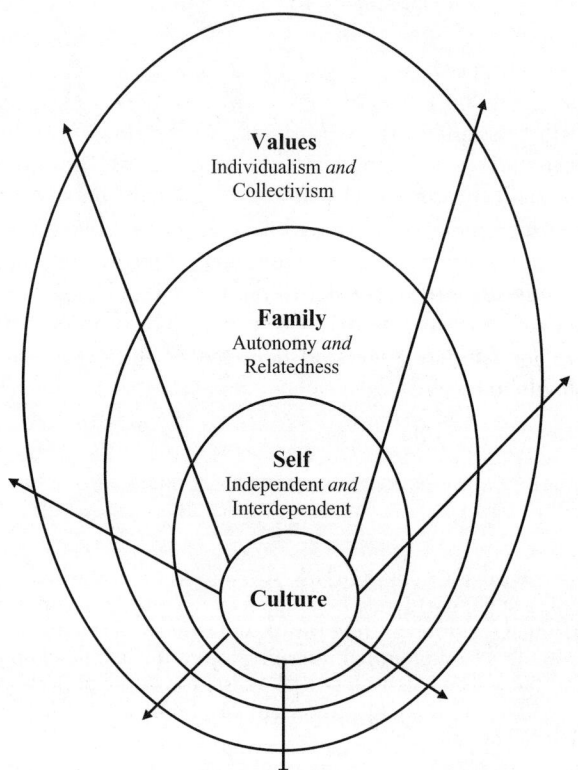

value system, contribute to the meaning of parent and adolescent conflict among Chinese American families.

The dimension of individualism–collectivism (IC) is one of the most widely studied aspects of culture (Hofstede, 1980; Triandis, 2001). Individualism refers to a value system that emphasizes the self, the "I," the autonomous individual, where individual needs take precedence over group (such as family) needs. Collectivism refers to a value system that emphasizes others, the "we," the interconnected individual within groups, where group needs take precedence over individual needs. Individualism–collectivism value systems are believed to correspond to both the family context and individuals' own sense of self and have been used as a way to explain cultural variations across many aspects of human development, including differences in parenting and socialization behaviors, beliefs, and goals. In the family context, IC parallels a perceived emphasis on autonomy or relatedness within the parent–child relationship (Kağitçibaşi, 2005). In terms of a sense of self, IC ostensibly facilitates the development of an independent or interdependent self-construal (Markus & Kitayama, 1991). Taken together, the cultural values of IC correspond to parenting practices focused on autonomy or relatedness aimed at fostering the development of an independent or an interdependent self (Figure 2.1). In this chapter, we focus on the constructs of autonomy and relatedness to reinterpret our views of parent–adolescent conflict in Chinese American families.

The dichotomous view of IC and autonomy versus relatedness is deeply embedded in our notions of parent–child relationships and child development. A common proposition is that in Western cultures (e.g., North America, Western Europe, Australia) a primary developmental goal that parents have for their children is to promote autonomy as one form of individualism. In contrast, in Eastern cultures (e.g., Asian countries), a primary developmental goal is to promote relatedness as an expression of collectivism. We know, however, that this dichotomous view of concepts and cultures is far too simplistic. Indeed, the either/or characterizations of IC and autonomy-relatedness have been soundly rejected, both conceptually and empirically (Kağitçibaşi, 2005; Matsumoto, 1999; Nsamenang, 2011; Okazaki & Saw, 2011; Oyserman, Coon, & Kemmelmeier, 2002; Smetana, 2002; Tamis-LeMonda et al., 2008).

Tamis-LeMonda et al. (2008) offer a provocative new framework that retains the theoretically useful aspects of IC without the limitations inherent in a static and polar model. In their model, parents' developmental goals for autonomy and relatedness exist simultaneously in all cultures, but relate to one another in various ways: conflicting (e.g., relatedness is emphasized over autonomy), additive (both are viewed as desirable), or functionally dependent (one is necessary for promoting the other). Tamis-LeMonda et al. (2008) emphasize that these relations can change depending on the situation, developmental period, and sociohistorical context. The authors note that for immigrant families, the changing relation between autonomy and relatedness may be especially challenging, as parents must deal with fulfilling both developmental goals in a different environment. Tamis-LeMonda and colleagues' model offers a useful way to understand the complex manifestations of behavior aligned with I and C. Such a model calls for research that examines the role of both I and C *within* a single cultural group. Accordingly, in this chapter we examine both notions of I (autonomy) and C (relatedness) within one population—Chinese American families.

Despite recent theoretical advances, the polar dichotomy of IC and autonomy-relatedness continues to play an important role in our understanding of child development and has led to two disparate literatures on family conflict during adolescence: everyday conflict and acculturation-based conflict. In our review of these literatures, we took notice of an implicit alignment with the polar conceptualization of IC. Everyday conflict, which has been studied primarily among European American families, is viewed as an assertion of autonomy from parents that is normative during adolescence (Laursen, Coy, & Collins, 1998; Steinberg & Morris, 2001). Acculturation-based conflict, which has been studied primarily among Asian- and Latino-heritage families (both characterized as emphasizing family interdependence), is viewed as a threat to relatedness with parents rather than the normative assertion of autonomy (Portes & Rumbaut, 2001). Thus, in contrast to everyday conflict, acculturation-based conflict tends to be viewed more negatively and is rarely considered to be developmentally normative or adaptive (e.g., Kwak, 2003; Portes & Rumbaut, 1996, 2001). As we will propose later in this chapter, it is possible that both types of conflict are normative and adaptive, but the existing literature generally aligns everyday conflict and acculturation-based conflict differentially, at least with regard to long-term development and well-being.

Although there is robust literature on both types of conflict, researchers have not systematically considered these two types of conflict together. Lacking in the literature, for example, is evidence on whether these types of conflict are conceptually distinct, and if so, how they are related, whether they uniquely predict adolescent adjustment, if they affect parent–child relationships in the same way, and if they serve different purposes and promote different developmental goals that parents have for their children. We attempt to address these shortcomings in this chapter. Our overarching goal, then, is to explore and integrate our knowledge of the two types of family conflict to arrive at a new understanding of what family conflict means for Chinese American adolescents and their parents.

Acculturation-Based Conflict and Everyday Conflict: Two Parallel Literatures

For adolescents in immigrant families, researchers have conceptualized parent–adolescent conflict as rooted in the acculturation process. Because adolescents tend to adopt the values and behaviors of the mainstream culture faster and more strongly than their parents (Cheung, Chudek, & Heine, 2011; Costigan & Dokis, 2006; Kwak, 2003; Lee, Choe, Kim, & Ngo, 2000; Phinney, Ong, & Madden, 2000), parents and adolescents may experience acculturation dissonance—a mismatch in their cultural values, attitudes, and beliefs (Portes & Rumbaut, 1996, 2001). This dissonance can be disturbing and lead to greater parent–adolescent conflict over core cultural beliefs (Juang, Syed, & Takagi, 2007; Kwak, 2003; Lee et al., 2000; Portes & Rumbaut, 1996, 2001; Qin, 2006). Thus, acculturation theorists propose that parents and adolescents engage in conflict primarily because of clashing cultural values. Rivera et al. (2008) have described this type of acculturation-based conflict for Latino-heritage families as "conflict that might arise because of the tension of fitting into the cultural norms of strong family ties and achieving more personal goals" (p. 363). Lee et al. (2000) have identified specific acculturation-based conflicts for Asian American youth centered around culturally salient issues such as respect for elders, academic achievement, and sacrificing personal goals for the sake of the family. Indeed, evidence suggests that acculturation-based conflict is a contributor to a variety of problems for Asian-heritage youth, including low self-esteem, anxiety, depressive symptoms, and somatization (Juang et al., 2007; Lee et al., 2000; Lim, Yeh, Liang, Lau, & McCabe, 2009; Qin, 2006). However, none of these studies have considered or tested whether acculturation-based conflict is temporary or possibly adaptive for promoting the developmental goals of autonomy or relatedness.

In contrast to literature on acculturation-based conflict, the bulk of research on normative "everyday" conflict (e.g., over household chores, schoolwork) has primarily focused on European American families (see Laursen et al., 1998, for a review). Further, everyday conflict has been explicitly related to the developmental goal of autonomy (Fuligni, 1998; Smetana, 2002; Steinberg & Morris, 2001). Smetana (2002) notes that in the early family conflict literature, finding that parents and adolescents engaged in conflict over everyday issues was somewhat of a surprise. Originally, researchers believed that parents and adolescents argued over more serious, deeper values. However, large-scale survey studies showed that parents and adolescents generally agreed on important values (Offer, 1969). Where they disagreed concerned social conventional issues, or "everyday" issues that were based on conventional (familial or societal) ways of doing things such as regarding homework, doing household chores, and what to wear. The finding that European American families tend to engage in conflict around everyday issues to a greater degree than deeper value-based issues led researchers to focus on how conflict over everyday issues was developmentally important. The emergence of research on immigrant families' adjustment to the United States helped revive the focus on values, as immigrant families occupy a unique context in which they are negotiating two or more potentially conflicting value systems. As a result, value-based conflict may occur more frequently within immigrant families, which may or may not coincide with conflict around everyday issues. Indeed, the literature of family conflict in immigrant families has seldom focused on everyday conflict, which is opposite of the literature with nonimmigrant families.

The few existing studies found that, in general, ethnic minority immigrant families (such as with Mexican, Chinese, and Filipino heritage), engaged in similar levels of everyday conflict as their European American counterparts (Chen, Greenberger, Lester, Dong, & Guo, 1998; Fuligni, 1998; Greenberger & Chen, 1996). Overall, for most adolescents of various cultural groups everyday conflict appears to be quite moderate. This type of conflict over everyday issues is viewed as normative, temporary, and functional, as it realigns the parent–adolescent relationship (Laursen, et al., 1998) and facilitates the development of autonomy (or individuation) for youth of various cultural backgrounds (Fuligni, 1998; Smetana, 2002; Steinberg & Morris, 2001; Yau & Smetana, 1996). Further, it is argued that this realignment ultimately establishes a parent–adolescent relationship that is "less contentious, more egalitarian, and less volatile" (Steinberg & Morris, 2001, p. 88). Thus, everyday conflict is viewed as normative and developmentally adaptive; in contrast, acculturation-based conflict is not.

In sum, the literature on everyday conflict, such as arguing over homework or doing household chores, suggests that these issues are relevant for most adolescents, regardless of immigrant status (Smetana, 2002). In contrast, the literature on acculturation-based conflict, or conflict rooted in differences over particular cultural values, attitudes, and beliefs, suggests that these issues may be relevant for immigrant adolescents specifically (Kwak, 2003; Portes & Rumbaut, 1996, 2001). Importantly, these two bodies of literature have demonstrated that both types of conflict are salient for Chinese-heritage adolescents. In contrast to everyday conflict, acculturation-based conflict has been viewed in a much more negative light. Although everyday and acculturation-based conflicts have been studied in Chinese American populations, researchers have not merged these two literatures to ask two important questions: "How are these two types of conflict related?" and "Do they each uniquely predict adolescent adjustment?" We address these questions now.

How Are Acculturation-Based and Everyday Conflict Related and Do They Contribute Uniquely to Adolescent Well-Being?

In previous analyses of Chinese American families using some of the same data reported in this chapter, we found that acculturation-based conflict and everyday conflict were positively correlated and change in parallel over time—if one increased, so did the other (Juang, Syed, & Cookston, 2012). The correlation between the two types of conflict, however, was moderate over time ($r = .44$, $p < .001$), suggesting that these are two distinct types of conflict. Furthermore, we found that the two types of conflict are *unique* predictors of psychological functioning. Specifically, greater acculturation-based conflict predicted greater anxiety/somatization, loneliness, depressive symptoms, and self-esteem over and above the contribution of everyday conflict, which also consistently predicted poorer well-being. We also found that acculturation-based conflict was more consistently linked to adolescent well-being compared to everyday conflict. For instance, the relation between acculturation-based conflict and adolescent well-being was a dynamic one—when conflict increased over a 2-year period, there was a synchronized decrease in well-being over a 2-year period. This synchronized change was not seen for everyday conflict and well-being.

Taken together, the results of our earlier work highlight the importance of considering how the acculturation process contributes to parent–adolescent conflict concerning everyday issues and core cultural values. Thus, family conflict in immigrant families should capture both "normative" everyday issues as well as conflict explicitly related to differences in cultural values between parents and children. Based on our finding that the two types of conflict are related but distinct, future research could examine more in-depth how these two types of conflict are linked. Researchers could, for instance, explore whether engaging in one type of conflict exacerbates engaging in another (testing for interaction effects), or whether one type of conflict precedes the development of the other. It could also be the case that greater parent–child acculturation discrepancies during late childhood set the stage for engaging in more everyday arguments during adolescence.

In this next section, we address two additional questions that have not yet been explored: "Do the two types of conflict affect parent–child relationships in the same way?" and "Do they potentially have different mechanisms that lead to well-being?" In other words, we examine whether the two types of conflict have different consequences for parenting and family cohesion, and if so, how this ultimately contributes to adolescent well-being.

Pathways to Well-Being: An Integration of the Family Conflict Literatures

Viewed as a dynamic interplay rather than either/or, the IC and autonomy-relatedness frameworks are useful for understanding why there may be different pathways to child well-being from everyday and acculturation-based conflict. As reviewed earlier, there are divergent views of how the two types of conflict will affect family relationships. Although there is evidence that greater everyday conflict relates to less closeness with parents among European Americans (Laursen et al., 1998) and less parental warmth among Chinese Americans (Chen et al., 1998) and African Americans (Costigan, Cauce, & Etchison, 2007), the everyday conflict literature has emphasized that moderate levels of this type of conflict are developmentally appropriate and do not have long-term consequences (Laursen et al., 1998). The emphasis in this literature is the facilitation of adolescents' autonomy development. In general, there is agreement that everyday conflict, for most adolescents, does not permanently harm family relationships.

In contrast, the acculturation-based conflict literature has highlighted the disruptiveness of this type of conflict to family relationships, warning that when parents and adolescents acculturate at a different pace and end up culturally incongruent (e.g., the adolescent does not have a strong orientation to Chinese culture while his or her parents do), there will be negative consequences for the family. Because of Chinese-heritage families' emphasis on relatedness (e.g., family obligation, filial piety), acculturation-based conflict may be especially detrimental to parent–child relationships and family cohesion (Lee at al., 2000). Kim and colleagues, for instance, showed that parents who experience greater acculturation dissonance with their children also show less supportive parenting practices in terms of less monitoring, warmth, and use of inductive reasoning (Kim, Chen, Li, Huang, & Moon, 2009; Weaver & Kim, 2008). These findings suggest that acculturation-based conflicts arising from a lack of shared cultural understanding between parents and children (acculturation dissonance) may undermine the quality of parenting. Similarly, Qin (2006) proposed that parents and children who experience acculturation dissonance develop *parallel dual frames of reference* for appropriate parent–child relationships. In some families, parents have a frame of reference that is based on the values of heritage culture, whereas their adolescents have a frame of reference based on the values of the majority culture. These differences in frames of reference (or lack of shared understanding) can lead to poorer parent–adolescent communication, feelings of distance, and even alienation between parents and children over time. Taken together, this previous work suggests that acculturation-based conflicts can impair the quality of parenting and family relationships and, ultimately, lead to poorer adolescent well-being.

Based on these two literatures, we propose that acculturation-based conflict would relate to poorer adolescent well-being primarily by affecting the quality of parenting and lessening family cohesion. Everyday conflict, on the other hand, would also be related to poorer adolescent well-being, but we expect this type of conflict would not affect the quality of parenting and family cohesion to the same extent as acculturation-based conflict. In empirical language, we expect that quality of parenting and family cohesion would be a more consistent mediator of the relation between acculturation-based conflict and adolescent well-being than for everyday conflict and well-being.

Two Longitudinal Studies: Testing Different Pathways to Well-Being for Two Types of Conflict

We draw upon two longitudinal studies of Chinese American families to test whether there are indeed different pathways to well-being depending on the type of conflict. The advantage of using two datasets is that it allows us to replicate findings as well as include a wider range of variables (measuring parenting, family, and adolescent well-being). Both studies collected data at two time points from adolescents residing in northern California; Study A took place in 2001 and 2003 (at mean age of 14.8 and 16.8 years), and Study B in 2002 and 2006 (at mean age of 13 and 17 years).

For this chapter, we included adolescent self-report data for all measures. Both datasets have the same measure of acculturation-based conflict. The 10-item acculturation-based conflict measure (Lee et al., 2000) includes culturally salient themes representing opposing parent–child views such as parents wanting adolescents to sacrifice personal interests for the sake of the family but adolescents feeling this is unfair, and adolescents doing well in school but parents' expectations always exceeding their performance. Each study used a different measure of everyday conflict, but both studies used measures that addressed "normative" issues during adolescence that were not culturally specific such as discussions over schoolwork and chores (see Table 2.1 for a summary of the samples and measures used in each study).

For the parenting and family variables (the mediators), Study A used one family cohesion measure and Study B used one quality of parent–adolescent relationship measure (adolescents' sense of alienation from parent) and four parenting measures (parental hostility, harsh parenting, parental control, and democratic parenting). With respect to adolescent well-being, Study A included four measures (depressive symptoms, somatization/anxiety, loneliness, and self-esteem) and Study B included two (depressive symptoms and delinquency). All indicators of well-being were assessed at both Times 1 and 2. Measures of conflict and parenting/family variables (mediators) were administered only at Time 2.

To test whether there were different pathways from the two types of conflict to adolescent well-being, we used path analysis and tested for mediation effects with MPlus 6.1 using maximum likelihood estimation (Muthén & Muthén, 2001). For each of the adolescent well-being measures, we specified a model whereby acculturation-based and everyday conflict predicted a mediator (one of the parenting and family variables), and the mediator predicted adolescent well-being. The direct effect from conflict to adolescent well-being was also included in the model. In all

Table 2.1. Summary of Two Longitudinal Studies of Chinese American Adolescents

	Study A (N = 274)	Study B (N = 444)
Mean age (SD)	14.8 years (.73) at T1, 16.8 (.77) at T2	13.0 years (.73) at T1, 17.05 (.80) at T2
Parent education	For mothers, 30% had less than a high school degree and 70% completed a high school degree or higher. For fathers, 38% had less than high school degree and 62% completed a high school degree or higher.	For mothers, 32% had less than a high school degree and 68% completed high school degree or higher. For fathers, 37% had less than a high school degree and 63% completed a high school degree or higher.
Gender	57% Female	54% Female
Generational status	70% U.S. born, 30% foreign-born	75% U.S. born, 25% foreign-born
Measures		
Acculturation-based family conflict	Asian American Family Conflict Scale-Likelihood (Lee et al., 2000; $\alpha = .87$)	Asian American Family Conflict Scale-Likelihood (Lee et al., 2000; $\alpha = .92$)
Everyday conflict	Issues Checklist – Frequency (Prinz, Foster, Kent, & O'Leary, 1979; $\alpha = .85$)	Intergenerational Conflict Inventory (Chung, 2001; $\alpha = .88$)
Depressive symptoms	Center for Epidemiological Studies-Depression (Radloff, 1977; $\alpha = .85$)	Center for Epidemiological Studies-Depression (Radloff, 1977; $\alpha = .91$)
Somatization/anxiety	Brief Symptom Inventory (Derogatis, 1993; $\alpha = .83$)	—
Loneliness	The Revised UCLA Loneliness Questionnaire (Russell, Peplau, & Cutrona, 1980; $\alpha = .89$)	—
Self-esteem	Rosenberg Self-Esteem scale (Rosenberg, 1989; $\alpha = .85$)	—
Delinquency	—	Youth Self Report (Achenbach, 1991; $\alpha = .68$)
Family cohesion	Family Cohesion subscale from the Family Adaptability and Cohesion Evaluation Scales II (Olson, Russell, & Sprenkle 1983; $\alpha = .84$).	—
Sense of alienation	—	Alienation subscale of Inventory of Parent and Peer Attachment (Armsden & Greenberg, 1987; $\alpha = .87$)
Parental hostility	—	Adapted from Iowa Youth and Families Project (Conger & Elder, 1994; $\alpha = .91$)
Harsh parenting	—	Adapted from Iowa Youth and Families Project (Conger & Elder, 1994; Kim & Ge, 2000; $\alpha = .77$)
Parent control	—	Psychological control (Barber, 1996; $\alpha = .91$)
Democratic parenting	—	Parenting Practices Questionnaire (Robinson, Mandleco, Olson, & Hart, 1995; $\alpha = .86$)

models, adolescent age, gender, generational status (U.S. born vs. foreign-born), parent education, and Time 1 baseline well-being (e.g., when predicting depressive symptoms at Time 2, the model included depressive symptoms at Time 1) were included as controls. Bootstrap analysis with 1,000 samples was used to test whether the mediated effects were significant (Preacher & Hayes, 2008). Based on the range of these mediated effect estimates, 95% confidence intervals for the distribution of the mediated effect estimates were calculated. Confidence intervals that do not include zero indicate that the mediated effect was significant at $p < .05$. Bootstrapping has the advantage of producing more-accurate Type I error rates and has more statistical power than single sample methods that assume a normal distribution for the mediated effect (MacKinnon, Lockwood, & Williams, 2004).

The results from both datasets show a consistent pattern: When both types of conflict are considered within the same model, the relationship between acculturation-based conflict and adolescent well-being is mediated by parenting and family variables while everyday conflict is not (see Table 2.2 and Figure 2.2). More specifically, greater acculturation-based conflict predicted more parent–child alienation, parental hostility, parental

Figure 2.2. Summary of findings integrated into a schematic model in which acculturation-based conflict and everyday conflict each uniquely predicts poorer adolescent well-being through different pathways. Acculturation-based conflict operates through family factors. On the basis of our findings, the mechanism for everyday conflict remains unknown, but tests of the model provide evidence against several parenting and family factors.

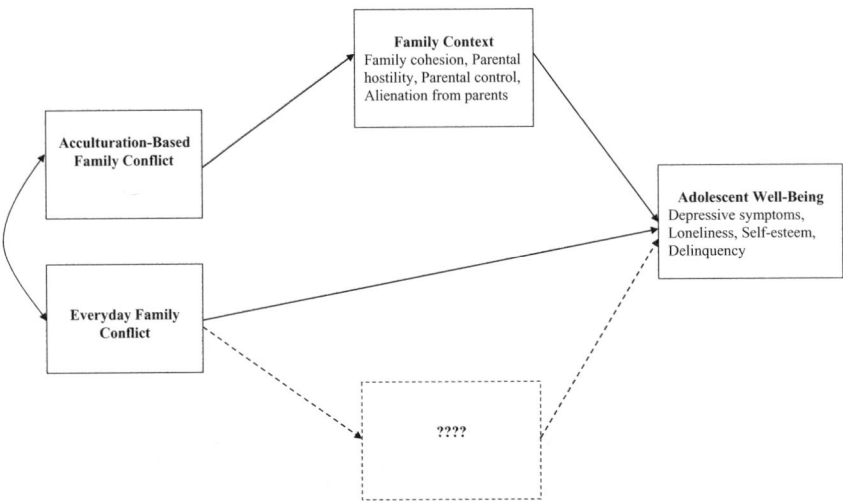

Table 2.2. Parenting/Family Variable Mediators of Acculturation-Based and Everyday Conflict to Adolescent Well-Being: Summary of Two Datasets

Mediator	Adolescent Adjustment	Acculturation-Based Conflict	95% CI	Everyday Conflict	95% CI
Family cohesion	Depressive symptoms	β = .072, p = .011	[.016, .128]	β = .038, p = .033	[.003, .073]
Family cohesion	Loneliness	β = .061, p = .019	[.010, .112]	β = .032, p = .048	[.000, .064]
Family cohesion	Somatization/anxiety	β = .035, p = .049	[.000, .070]	β = .018, p = .108	[−.004, .041]
Family cohesion	Self-esteem	β = −.067, p = .014	[−.065, −.007]	β = −.035, p = .047	[−.042, .000]
Sense of alienation	Depressive symptoms	β = .198, p = .019	[.033, .363]	β = .006, p = .733	[−.028, .040]
Parental hostility	Depressive symptoms	β = .121, p = .028	[.013, .230]	β = .009, p = .476	[−.015, .033]
Harsh parenting	Depressive symptoms	β = .036, p = .073	[−.003, .076]	β = .008, p = .331	[−.008, .023]
Parental control	Depressive symptoms	β = .129, p = .029	[.013, .246]	β = .031, p = .066	[−.002, .064]
Democratic parenting	Depressive symptoms	β = .057, p = .067	[−.004, .119]	β = .011, p = .183	[−.005, .026]
Sense of alienation	Delinquency	β = .090, p = .034	[.007, .174]	β = .002, p = .859	[−.016, .019]
Parental hostility	Delinquency	β = .064, p = .068	[−.001, .133]	β = .005, p = .475	[−.009, .020]
Harsh parenting	Delinquency	β = .052, p = .048	[.000, .103]	β = .012, p = .287	[−.010, .033]
Parental control	Delinquency	β = .079, p = .049	[.000, .158]	β = .021, p = .093	[−.004, .046]
Democratic parenting	Delinquency	β = .081, p = .037	[.005, .157]	β = .011, p = .141	[−.005, .039]

Note: Adolescent age, gender, generational status, parent education, and well-being assessed at Time 1 were controlled for in these analyses using Mplus testing indirect (mediated) effects. Models with a significant indirect effect of conflict to adolescent adjustment through a parenting/family variable are bolded. CI = confidence interval.

control, less democratic parenting, and less family cohesion. The negative parenting and family variables in turn predicted poorer adolescent well-being (greater depressive symptoms, somatization/anxiety, loneliness, delinquency, and lower self-esteem). In contrast, greater everyday family conflict showed primarily direct effects to poorer adolescent well-being (and only one indirect effect). In sum, acculturation-based conflict is more closely linked to parenting and family processes than everyday conflict, suggesting that arguing about core cultural values has more negative consequences for quality of parenting, parent–adolescent relationships, and family cohesion more so than arguing about everyday issues.

One strength of our analysis is that we tested our mediated model with two separate datasets. The fact that we found similar patterns in both datasets bolsters the argument that acculturation-based conflict may be detrimental to adolescent well-being through its association with parenting and family cohesion. What accounts for the link between everyday conflict and adolescent well-being remains unclear, but the current analysis suggests that everyday conflict does not pose the same threat to the family environment as does acculturation-based conflict, indicating that these two forms of conflict evidence different pathways to well-being.

Our findings support the notion that the acculturation process for immigrant parents and adolescents can be challenging, leading to greater distress and maladjustment for family members. Our mediation analyses clarify how this might happen—acculturation-based conflicts are linked to poorer parenting, more distant parent–adolescent relationships, and less family closeness, and these more negative family relationships predict poorer adolescent adjustment. Why is it the case that acculturation-based conflict is more tightly linked with family relationships than everyday conflict? Acculturation-based conflict measures may be better at assessing conflict in Chinese American families because they identify culturally salient themes unavailable in everyday conflict measures. Higher scores on the acculturation-based conflict measure represent parents and adolescents who are clashing on core cultural values, which may be disturbing for parents if they sense their adolescents are rejecting values they deem important. However, we need longitudinal data to uncover how this unfolds in young adulthood—Do acculturation-based conflicts foreshadow a continued, conflictual parent–adolescent relationship in young adulthood? Or, as with everyday conflict, are these conflicts temporary and even functional? If everyday conflict literature is any indication, acculturation-based conflict, while detrimental to family relations in the short-term, may not necessarily be detrimental in the long-term. We discuss this possibility in the last section of the chapter.

Based on Turiel's social domain theory (1983), Smetana's (1988, 2002) social domain perspective on family conflict proposes that one of the main reasons why adolescents and parents engage in conflict is that they tend to view the same issue through different lenses: Adolescents are more likely to view an issue as a personal concern whereas parents are more likely to view an issue as a social conventional concern. The crux of the disagreement, then, is divergent perceptions of who has the authority to decide what is appropriate. Although Smetana and colleagues have found that parents and adolescents diverge in their views of authority in both European American families and Hong Kong Chinese families (Smetana, 1988, 2002; Yau & Smetana, 1996), these divergent views may be heightened for immigrant Chinese American families and especially regarding acculturation-based issues. Consider, for example, the issue of respect. One of the items in the Asian American Family Conflict Scale (Lee et al., 2000) is "Your parents demand that you always show respect for elders, but you believe in showing respect only if they deserve it." Probably for most Chinese-heritage parents, not showing respect to elders may be a social conventional or even moral transgression. Their U.S.-born children, on the other hand, may view this as a personal transgression. Indeed, Smetana (2002) has argued that cultures vary in the range of issues that are considered under one's personal jurisdiction—some cultures will have a broader range than others. For Chinese American families, then, holding different viewpoints of authority—especially in relation to core cultural values of respect, achievement, and proper behavior—may undermine family relationships.

From an acculturation perspective, a slightly different interpretation is that Chinese American parents and adolescents hold parallel dual frames of reference (Qin, 2006) concerning the content of the social convention. Parents' frame of reference for what is conventional (and thus acceptable) regarding the issue of respect may be rooted more in traditional Chinese culture. In contrast, adolescents' frame of reference for what is conventional (and thus acceptable) regarding the issue of respect may be rooted more in mainstream American culture. Either way, from a social domain approach or acculturation perspective, parents and adolescents with unshared views in authority and/or values held, may have strained relationships that ultimately lead to poorer adolescent well-being.

In the end, what is considered an "everyday" versus "acculturation-based" conflict may be difficult to disentangle. We have argued, however, that everyday conflict has been traditionally conceived of as disagreements about relatively minor issues such as homework or chores (Smetana, 2002), whereas acculturation-based conflict has been conceived of as disagreements about more serious issues such as core cultural values (Portes & Rumbaut, 1996, 2001). We have also argued that the two types of conflict may be distinct, based on evidence that the two types of conflict uniquely predict several dimensions of well-being, and, are linked to well-being via different mechanisms, or pathways. Accordingly, an understanding of both types of conflicts is relevant and useful for advancing our understanding of parent–adolescent conflict among Chinese immigrant families.

Future Research on Family Conflict with Chinese Immigrant Families

In our analysis of Chinese American families, we found that parent–adolescent conflict, especially concerning issues arising specifically from the acculturation process, is challenging for adolescent adjustment. We also found evidence for differential pathways that explain why family conflict is associated with poorer adolescent adjustment. Our findings point the way for several future areas of inquiry.

General versus Domain-Specific Constructs. One implication from our findings is the need for domain specificity of constructs—both in type of conflict and type of parenting and family variables of interest. Our findings suggest that acculturation-based conflict may negatively affect family relationships whereas everyday conflict may not. The need for domain specific models of conflict is supported by Costigan and Dokis's work (2006) showing that parent–adolescent discrepancies along the Canadian dimension of acculturation did not relate to adolescent well-being, but discrepancies along the Chinese dimension (parents endorsing Chinese values and beliefs more than their children) did. The authors argue that parents most likely expect discrepancies in the Canadian dimension and encourage their children to adopt Canadian culture for their children to succeed. In contrast, parents and adolescents who cannot see eye to eye concerning their heritage culture is problematic (see also Updegraff, Umaña-Taylor, Perez-Brena, & Pflieger [this volume] for relevant findings concerning cultural orientation discrepancies and adjustment). Thus, different areas of conflict may not have the same impact on adolescent well-being. Qin, Chang, Han, and Chee's (this volume) qualitative approach identifies other domains of acculturation-based conflicts such as how parental educational pressure is communicated and discrepancies in parents' and adolescents' attitudes toward other races. Specifying the type of conflict and potential mediator(s) provides a stronger explanatory model for understanding pathways to adolescent well-being.

Focusing on specific topics of conflict may also be useful. In both of our datasets (mirroring Lee et al.'s 2000 study with Asian American college students), the top two acculturation-based conflicts were "Your parents always compare you to others, but you want them to accept you for being yourself," and "You have done well in school, but your parents' academic expectations always exceed your performance." For Chinese-heritage individuals, pressures to live up to high expectations academically and constant comparisons to others (who are doing well) appear to be central concerns for both adolescents and emerging adults. Other studies have documented the immense academic pressures that Chinese American parents place on their children. Qin's (2006, 2008) ethnographic studies of Chinese American adolescents and their families showed that adolescents were often overwhelmed by these high expectations. Because adolescents perceived their parents as caring only for their school performance and ignoring other aspects of their lives, adolescents and parents communicated less over time and became increasingly distant and alienated from one another. For intervention and prevention purposes, it will be important to focus on these two acculturation-based conflict issues as they are the most common. Future research could examine how and why parents and adolescents come to have such discrepant viewpoints concerning academic performance and social comparisons.

When Is Family Conflict Adaptive? One limitation to our findings is that we solely focused on the negative impact of family conflict. Although most studies (including ours) have consistently found that conflict is related to negative adolescent well-being, a few studies have found otherwise. In some immigrant families, family conflict enriched family relationships by improving communication and promoting better understanding among family members (Stuart, Ward, Jose, & Narayanan, 2010). Thus, while conflict has been conceptualized primarily as important for promoting autonomy in the adolescent, it may also promote relatedness, a concept usually thought of (erroneously) as the opposite of autonomy (Tamis-LeMonda et al., 2008). Future research should examine more of the positive aspects of conflict beyond a general promotion of autonomy. For example, in the identity literature, conflict is generally discussed positively, as conflicts allow individuals to reflect on who they are and modify their identities in light of their current and perceived future goals (e.g., Bruner, 1990). Indeed, Smetana (2008) has recently called for a focus on the distinction between "constructive" versus "destructive" conflict. In other words, future research should focus on conflict that may be developmentally appropriate and that promotes certain developmental goals versus conflict that does more harm to family relationships.

It is still not clear whether acculturation-based conflict is more constructive or destructive. In our chapter, we could not directly address this. One way to find out is to focus on how conflicts are resolved. One step in this direction is Cookston et al.'s (this volume) chapter on who adolescents turn to to make sense of conflict with parents. Smetana (2008) argues that conflict resolution and not the actual conflict itself may be more consequential for parent–adolescent relationships and adolescent functioning. We know that in some Chinese American families, conflict-resolving strategies are not optimal. Qin and colleagues' (2006, current volume) work found that yelling, ignoring, and distancing were common ways that adolescents and parents dealt with conflict. Researchers could explore whether there are differences in intensity or emotionality of acculturation-based versus everyday conflict, whether there are differences in how these two types of conflict are usually resolved, and how conflict resolution contributes to whether conflict can be adaptive, maladaptive, or both.

The Consequences of Family Conflict Beyond Adolescence. The long-term impact of family conflict (particularly acculturation-based) on youth adjustment is unclear given the lack of longitudinal studies that have followed adolescents through young adulthood and beyond. Although it has been argued that moderate, everyday conflict does not have long-term negative consequences on the adolescent or family, we do not know if this is true for acculturation-based conflict, especially if this type of conflict is disruptive to family relationships. There is some evidence, however, that acculturation-based conflict in adolescence, similar to everyday conflict, may not have negative long-term consequences—at least for some families. A qualitative study of Korean American college students, for instance, found that a majority reported acculturation-related conflicts with parents during adolescence concerning high academic pressures and expectations, and communication difficulties (Kang, Okazaki, Abelmann, Kim-Prieto, & Shanshan, 2010). However, during emerging adulthood, the college students saw their parents differently and could appreciate more fully their parents' behaviors even though they disapproved of and resented the way they parented when they were younger. Kang et al. (2010) conclude that although relationships between parents and adolescents were often difficult, by emerging adulthood a majority of Korean Americans could reconcile their difficult relationships and come to a greater understanding and appreciation of their parents. In other words, they were able to consider their parents' perspective, empathize, and reinterpret conflicts with parents in a constructive way. We know that with age comes maturation in perspective taking and a greater ability to understand another person's intentions and beliefs (Choudhury, Blakemore, & Charman, 2006; McLean & Thorne, 2003). Thus, young adults' perspectives on acculturation-based conflict, like everyday conflict, may be reinterpreted in a less negative, possibly even adaptive way, as children get older. Future studies (using both quantitative and qualitative approaches) could examine how youth make meaning of family conflict as they get older and focus on implications for their current relationships with their parents and their long-term adjustment.

Finally, studies could also focus on other ways that acculturation-based conflict may be adaptive in the long-term, for instance by helping adolescents and young adults clarify their own values and behaviors (promoting autonomy) to arrive at a better understanding of themselves and their parents (promoting relatedness). Using Tamis-LeMonda et al.'s (2008) dynamic IC framework, it may be the case that by young adulthood, parents' developmental goals have shifted in balance (e.g., moving from emphasizing relatedness to emphasizing both autonomy and relatedness) and manner of coexistence (e.g., moving from perceiving autonomy and relatedness as conflicting to functionally dependent). No research has yet examined how parents' developmental goals of autonomy and relatedness coexist and shift over time. Future research that examines how the meaning and consequences of family conflict changes within this dynamic IC framework is needed.

Conclusion

We began the chapter with the notion of turning Bronfenbrenner's graphic model inside out—where the outer circle of culture is the center point for understanding family dynamics such as family conflict. By taking a cultural perspective and focusing on the cultural dimensions of IC, we argued that researchers have highlighted everyday conflict as important for the promotion of an individualistic orientation (autonomy) while acculturation-based conflict for potentially diminishing a collectivistic orientation (relatedness). Based on our integration of these two literatures on conflict, our analysis of two datasets, Smetana's (2002) social domain approach and Tamis-LeMonda et al.'s (2008) dynamic IC theoretical framework, we argue that a deeper understanding of both types of conflict are important for Chinese American adolescent development. Although the two types of conflict are related and uniquely predict poorer adolescent well-being, only acculturation-based conflict is linked to poorer well-being via parenting and family relationships. Implications for family interventions would be to focus on acculturation-based conflicts to prevent family relationships from eroding. Future research should continue to address how adolescents make meaning of everyday and acculturation-based conflict, follow adolescents through to young adulthood, and focus on conflict resolution. By exploring these aspects of conflict more thoroughly and longitudinally, we might find that, as with everyday conflict, moderate levels of acculturation-based conflict during adolescence is normative, temporary, and, ultimately, developmentally adaptive in terms of promoting both autonomy and relatedness.

References

Achenbach, T. (1991). *Manual for the Youth Self-Report and 1991 Profile*. Burlington, VT: University of Vermont, Department of Psychology.

Armsden, G. C., & Greenberg, M. T. (1987). The Inventory of Parent and Peer Attachment: Individual differences and their relationship to psychological well-being in adolescence. *Journal of Youth and Adolescence, 16*, 427–454. doi: 10.1007/BF02202939

Barber, B. K. (1996). Parental psychological control: Revisiting a neglected construct. *Child Development, 67*, 3296–3319. doi: 10.1111/1467-8624.ep9706244861

Bronfenbrenner, U. (1979). *The ecology of human development*. Cambridge, MA: Harvard University Press.

Bruner, J. (1990). *Acts of meaning*. Cambridge, MA: Harvard University Press.

Chen, C., Greenberger, E., Lester, J., Dong, Q., & Guo, M.-S. (1998). A cross-cultural study of family and peer correlates of adolescent misconduct. *Developmental Psychology, 34*(4), 770–781. doi: 10.1037/0012-1649.34.4.770

Cheung, B. Y., Chudek, M., & Heine, S. J. (2011). Evidence for a sensitive period for acculturation: Younger immigrants report acculturating at a faster rate. *Psychological Science, 22*(2), 147–152.

Choudhury, S., Blakemore, S.-J., & Charman, T. (2006). Social cognitive development during adolescence. *Social Cognitive and Affective Neuroscience, 1*(3), 165–174. doi: 10.1093/scan/nsl024

Chung, R.H.G. (2001). Gender, ethnicity, and acculturation in intergenerational conflict of Asian American college students. *Cultural Diversity and Ethnic Minority Psychology, 7*, 376–386. doi: 10.1037/1099-9809.7.4.376

Conger, R. D., & Elder, G. H., Jr. (1994). *Families in troubled times.* New York, NY: DeGruyter.

Cookston, J. T., Olide, A. F., Adams, M. A., Fabricius, W. V., Parke, R. D. (2012). Guided cognitive reframing of adolescent–father conflict: Who Mexican American and European American adolescents seek and why. In L. P. Juang & A. J. Umaña-Taylor (Eds.), *Family conflict among Chinese- and Mexican-origin adolescents and their parents in the U.S. New Directions for Child and Adolescent Development, 135*, 83–103.

Costigan, C. L., Cauce, A. M., & Etchison, K. (2007). Changes in African American mother-daughter relationships during adolescence: Conflict, autonomy, and warmth. In B. J. R. Leadbeater & N. Way (Eds.), *Urban girls revisited: Building strengths* (pp. 177–201). New York, NY: New York University Press.

Costigan, C. L., & Dokis, D. P. (2006). Relations between parent-child acculturation differences and adjustment within immigrant Chinese families. *Child Development, 77*(5), 1252–1267. doi: 10.1111/j.1467-8624.2006.00932.x

Derogatis L. R. (1993). *Brief Symptom Inventory: Administration, scoring, and procedures manual.* 4th ed. Minneapolis, MN: National Computer Systems.

Fuligni, A. J. (1998). Authority, autonomy, and parent–adolescent conflict and cohesion: A study of adolescents from Mexican, Chinese, Filipino, and European backgrounds. *Developmental Psychology, 34*(4), 782–792. doi: 10.1037/0012-1649.34.4.782

Goodnow, J. J. (2011). Merging cultural and psychological accounts of family contexts. In L. A. Jensen (Ed.), *Bridging cultural and developmental approaches to psychology: New syntheses in theory, research, and policy* (pp. 73–91). New York, NY: Oxford University Press.

Greenberger, E., & Chen, C. (1996). Perceived family relationships and depressed mood in early and late adolescence: A comparison of European and Asian Americans. *Developmental Psychology, 32*(4), 707–716. doi: 10.1037/0012-1649.32.4.707

Hofstede, G. (1980). *Culture's consequence: International differences in work-related values.* Beverly Hills, CA: Sage.

Juang, L. P., Syed, M., & Cookston, J. T. (2012). *Trajectories and mental health correlates of family conflict among Chinese American adolescents.* Manuscript under review.

Juang, L. P., Syed, M., & Takagi, M. (2007). Intergenerational discrepancies of parental control among Chinese American families: Links to family conflict and adolescent depressive symptoms. *Journal of Adolescence, 30*(6), 965–975. doi: 10.1016/j.adolescence.2007.01.004

Kağitçibaşi, C. (2005). Autonomy and relatedness in cultural context: Implications for self and family. *Journal of Cross-Cultural Psychology, 36*(4), 403–422. doi: 10.1177/0022022105275959

Kang, H., Okazaki, S., Abelmann, N., Kim-Prieto, C., & Shanshan, L. (2010). Redeeming immigrant parents: How Korean American emerging adults reinterpret their childhood. *Journal of Adolescent Research, 25*(3), 441–464. doi: 10.1177/0743558410361371

Kim, S. Y., Chen, Q., Li, J., Huang, X., & Moon, U. J. (2009). Parent–child acculturation, parenting, and adolescent depressive symptoms in Chinese immigrant families. *Journal of Family Psychology, 23*(3), 426–437. doi: 10.1037/a0016019

Kim, S. Y., & Ge, X. (2000). Parenting practices and adolescent depressive symptoms in Chinese American families. *Journal of Family Psychology, 14*, 420–435. doi: 10.1037/0893-3200.14.3.420

Kwak, K. (2003). Adolescents and their parents: A review of intergenerational family relations for immigrant and non-immigrant families. *Human Development, 46*(2–3), 115–136. doi: 10.1159/000068581

Laursen, B., Coy, K. C., & Collins, W. A. (1998). Reconsidering changes in parent–child conflict across adolescence: A meta-analysis. *Child Development, 69*(3), 817–832. doi: 10.2307/1132206

Lee, R. M., Choe, J., Kim, G., & Ngo, V. (2000). Construction of the Asian American family conflicts scale. *Journal of Counseling Psychology, 47*(2), 211–222. doi: 10.1037/0022-0167.47.2.211

Lim, S.-L., Yeh, M., Liang, J., Lau, A. S., & McCabe, K. (2009). Acculturation gap, intergenerational conflict, parenting style, and youth distress in immigrant Chinese American families. *Marriage & Family Review, 45*(1), 84–106. doi: 10.1080/01494920802537530

MacKinnon, D. P., Lockwood, C. M., & Williams, J. (2004). Confidence limits for the indirect effect: Distribution of the product and resampling methods. *Multivariate Behavioral Research, 39*(1), 99–128. doi: 10.1207/s15327906mbr3901_4

Markus, H. R., & Kitayama, S. (1991). Culture and the self: Implications for cognition, emotion, and motivation. *Psychological Review, 98*(2), 224–253. doi: 10.1037/0033-295x.98.2.224

Matsumoto, D. (1999). Culture and self: An empirical assessment of Markus and Kitayama's theory of independent and interdependednt self-construal. *Asian Journal of Social Psychology, 2*(3), 289–310. doi: 10.1111/1467-839x.00042

Muthén, L. K., & Muthén, B. (2001). *Mplus user's guide*. Los Angeles, CA: Muthén & Muthén.

McLean, K. C., & Thorne, A. (2003). Late adolescents' self-defining memories about relationships. *Developmental Psychology, 39*(4), 635–645. doi:10.1037/0012-1649.39.4.635

Nsamenang, A. B. (2011). The culturalization of developmental trajectories: A perspective on African childhoods and adolescences. In L. A. Jensen (Ed.), *Bridging cultural and developmental approaches to psychology: New syntheses in theory, research, and policy* (pp. 235–254). New York, NY: Oxford University Press.

Offer, D. (1969). *The psychological world of the teenager*. New York, NY: Basic Books.

Okazaki, S., & Saw, A. (2011). Culture in Asian American community psychology: Beyond the East–West binary. *American Journal of Community Psychology, 47*(1–2), 144–156. doi: 10.1007/s10464-010-9368-z

Olson, D. H., Russell, C. S., & Sprenkle, D. H. (1983). Circumplex Model of marital and family systems: VI. Theoretical update. *Family Process, 22*(1), 69–83. doi: 10.1111/j.1545-5300.1983.00069.x

Oyserman, D., Coon, H. M., & Kemmelmeier, M. (2002). Rethinking individualism and collectivism: Evaluation of theoretical assumptions and meta-analyses. *Psychological Bulletin, 128*(1), 3–72. doi: 10.1037/0033-2909.128.1.3

Phinney, J. S., Ong, A., & Madden, T. (2000). Cultural values and intergenerational value discrepancies in immigrant and non-immigrant families. *Child Development, 71*(2), 528–539. doi: 10.1111/1467-8624.00162

Portes, A., & Rumbaut, R. (1996). *Immigrant America: A portrait*. Berkeley, CA: University of California Press.

Portes, A., & Rumbaut, R. (2001). *Legacies: The story of the immigrant second generation*. Berkeley, CA: University of California Press.

Preacher, K. J., & Hayes, A. F. (2008). Asymptotic and resampling strategies for assessing and comparing indirect effects in multiple mediator models. *Behavior Research Methods, 40*(3), 879–891. doi: 10.3758/brm.40.3.879

Prinz, R. J., Foster, S. L., Kent, R. N., & O'Leary, K. D. (1979). Multivariate assessment of conflict in distressed and nondistressed mother–adolescent dyads. *Journal of Applied Behavioral Analysis. 12,* 691–700.

Qin, D. B. (2006). "Our child doesn't talk to us anymore": Alienation in immigrant Chinese families. *Anthropology & Education Quarterly, 37*(2), 162–179. doi: 10.1525/aeq.2006.37.2.162

Qin, D. B. (2008). Doing well vs. feeling well: Understanding family dynamics and the psychological adjustment of Chinese immigrant adolescents. *Journal of Youth and Adolescence, 37*(1), 22–35. doi: 10.1007/s10964-007-9220-4

Qin, D. B., Chang, T-F., Han E-J., & Chee, G. (2012). Conflicts and communication between high-achieving Chinese American adolescents and their parents. In L. P. Juang & A. J. Umaña-Taylor (Eds.), *Family conflict among Chinese- and Mexican-origin adolescents and their parents in the U.S. New Directions for Child and Adolescent Development, 135,* 35–57.

Radloff, L. S. (1977). The CES-D scale: A self-report depression scale for research in the general population. *Applied Psychological Measurement, 1*(3), 385–401. doi: 10.1177/014662167700100306

Rivera, F. I., Guarnaccia, P. J., Mulvaney-Day, N., Lin, J. Y., Torres, M., & Alegría, M. (2008). Family cohesion and its relationship to psychological distress among latino groups. *Hispanic Journal of Behavioral Sciences, 30*(3), 357–378. doi: 10.1177/0739986308318713

Robinson, C. C., Mandleco, B., Olson, S. F., & Hart, C. H. (1995). Authoritative, authoritarian, and permissive parenting practices: Development of a new measure. *Psychological Reports, 77,* 819–830. doi: 10.2466/pr0.1995.77.3.819

Rosenberg, M. (1989). *Society and the adolescent self-image* (rev. ed.). Middletown, CT: Wesleyan University Press.

Russell, D., Peplau, L. A., & Cutrona, C. E. (1980). The Revised UCLA Loneliness Scale: Concurrent and discriminant validity evidence. *Journal of Personality and Social Psychology, 39*(3), 472–480. doi: 10.1037/0022-3514.39.3.472

Smetana, J. G. (1988). Adolescents' and parents' conceptions of parental authority. *Child Development, 59*(2), 321–335. doi: 10.2307/1130313

Smetana, J. G. (2002). Culture, autonomy, and personal jurisdiction in adolescent-parent relationships. In R. V. Kail & H. W. Reese (Eds.), *Advances in child development and behavior* (Vol. 2, pp. 51–87). San Diego, CA: Academic Press.

Steinberg, L., & Morris, A. S. (2001). Adolescent development. *Annual Review of Psychology, 52,* 83–110. doi: 10.1146/annurev.psych.52.1.83

Stuart, J., Ward, C., Jose, P. E., & Narayanan, P. (2010). Working with and for communities: A collaborative study of harmony and conflict in well-functioning, acculturating families. *International Journal of Intercultural Relations, 34*(2), 114–126. doi: 10.1016/j.ijintrel.2009.11.004

Tamis-LeMonda, C. S., Way, N., Hughes, D., Yoshikawa, H., Kalman, R. K., & Niwa, E. Y. (2008). Parents' goals for children: The dynamic coexistence of individualism and collectivism in cultures and individuals. *Social Development, 17*(1), 183–209.

Triandis, H. C. (2001). Individualism-collectivism and personality. *Journal of Personality, 69*(6), 907–924. doi: 10.1111/1467-6494.696169

Turiel, E. (1983). *The development of social knowledge: Morality and convention.* Cambridge, England: Cambridge University Press.

Updegraff, K. A., Umaña-Taylor, A. J., Perez-Brena, N., & Pflieger, J. (2012). Mother–daughter conflict and adjustment in Mexican-origin families: Exploring the role of family and sociocultural context. In L. P. Juang & A. J. Umaña-Taylor (Eds.), *Family conflict among Chinese- and Mexican-origin adolescents and their parents in the U.S. New Directions for Child and Adolescent Development, 135,* 59–81.

Weaver, S. R., & Kim, S. Y. (2008). A person-centered approach to studying the linkages among parent-child differences in cultural orientation, supportive parenting, and adolescent depressive symptoms in Chinese American families. *Journal of Youth and Adolescence, 37*(1), 36–49. doi: 10.1007/s10964-007-9221-3

Yau, J., & Smetana, J. G. (1996). Adolescent–parent conflict among Chinese adolescents in Hong Kong. *Child Development, 67*(3), 1262–1275. doi: 10.2307/1131891

LINDA P. JUANG *is a lecturer in the Department of Psychological and Brain Sciences at the University of California at Santa Barbara. E-mail: juang@psych.ucsb.edu, webpage: http://www.psych.ucsb.edu/people/faculty/juang/index.php*

MOIN SYED *is an assistant professor of psychology at the University of Minnesota. E-mail: moin@umn.edu, webpage: http://www.psych.umn.edu/people/faculty/syed.html*

JEFFREY T. COOKSTON *is an associate professor of psychology at San Francisco State University. E-mail: cookston@sfsu.edu, webpage: http://bss.sfsu.edu/devpsych/jcookston/*

YIJIE WANG *is a doctoral student in the Department of Human Development and Family Sciences at The University of Texas at Austin. E-mail: yiwang@prc.utexas.edu, webpage: http://he.utexas.edu/directory/wang-yijie*

SU YEONG KIM *is an assistant professor of human development and family sciences at The University of Texas at Austin. E-mail: sykim@prc.utexas.edu, webpage: http://he.utexas.edu/directory/kim-su-yeong*

> Qin, D. B., Chang, T-F., Han, E-J., & Chee, G. (2012). Conflicts and communication between high-achieving Chinese American adolescents and their parents. In L. P. Juang & A. J. Umaña-Taylor (Eds.), *Family conflict among Chinese- and Mexican-origin adolescents and their parents in the U.S. New Directions for Child and Adolescent Development,* 135, 35–57.

3

Conflicts and Communication Between High-Achieving Chinese American Adolescents and Their Parents

Desiree Baolian Qin, Tzu-Fen Chang, Eun-Jin Han, Grace Chee

Abstract

Drawing on in-depth interview data collected on 18 high-achieving Chinese American students, the authors examine domains of acculturation-based conflicts, parent and child internal conflicts, and conflict resolution in their families. Their analyses show that well-established negative communication patterns in educational expectations, divergent attitudes toward other races and country of origin, and cultural and language barriers contributed to parent–child conflicts. Their findings also illustrate important internal conflicts both adolescents and parents had along the cultural tightrope of autonomy and relatedness. Finally, the vertical in-group conflict resolution style that was evidenced in youths' accounts raises questions about cultural differences in constructive versus destructive conflict resolution styles. © 2012 Wiley Periodicals, Inc.

This study is funded by the William T Grant Foundation.

On January 8, 2011, the *Wall Street Journal* published an excerpt of Yale Law School professor Amy Chua's new book, *Battle Hymn of the Tiger Mother*, with a provocative title, "Why Chinese Mothers Are Superior" (Chua, 2011). In the book, Chua described in detail her endeavors to push her two daughters to succeed, denying them social life, sleepovers, and play dates and making frequent threats to motivate her daughters to perform better in their respective musical instruments. Indeed, her daughters are high achieving, winning multiple highly competitive contests. Her older daughter, Sophia, played at Carnegie Hall at age 15 and is currently attending an Ivy League university. Chua's depictions and the ensuing unparalleled media attention thrust Asian American parents into the limelight, their parenting debated and contested throughout the media and on social network sites. In these discussions, many are curious about the real-life experiences of high-achieving Chinese American children growing up with tiger mothers like Chua. In this chapter, we describe our attempts to gain a more in-depth understanding of the experiences of high-achieving Chinese American students by identifying salient domains of conflicts between parents and adolescents in these families, uncovering parents' and adolescents' internal conflicts, and examining how adolescents perceived the resolution of such conflicts in their families.

Traditional parent–child interactions in Asian American families are dictated largely by Confucian ethics and place parents and children in a vertical, hierarchical relationship (Tu, 1976). This positioning suppresses conflicts and, when conflicts do occur, prescribes specific resolution styles in Chinese families. However, after migration, cultural differences between parents and children (i.e., an acculturation gap) may create additional domains of conflict as well as influence how conflicts are resolved in Chinese American families (Ho, Chen, & Chiu, 1991; Juang, Syed, Cookston, Wang, & Kim, this volume). Scholars have identified some key domains of conflict salient to Chinese-heritage families that are particularly sensitive to the acculturation process including academic expectations, decision-making, parental expression of love, and respect (e.g., Costigan & Dokis, 2006; Crane, Ngai, Larson, & Hafen, 2005; Lee, Choe, Kim, & Ngo, 2000; Wu & Chao, 2005). A few studies have also been conducted to examine conflict resolution styles in Chinese American families (e.g., Lee, Su, & Yoshida, 2005; Okubo, Yeh, Lin, Fujita, & Shea, 2007). However, the study of parent–child conflict has been limited by its almost exclusive dependence on quantitative methods that examine the main domains and resolution styles, but not the dynamic processes underlying the main domains and resolution styles. Quantitative methodologies such as standardized surveys are also limited by their reliance on previously established domains (Way & Hamm, 2005) and resolution styles of conflicts. As a result, we do not have a full understanding of how these domains interact with each other, and how they may lead to elevated conflicts in immigrant families. In particular, in the description of conflicts between immigrant parents and their adolescents, parents and children are often depicted as coming from polarized, completely incompatible perspectives, e.g., children want more independence while parents want more obedience (Kwak, 2003). We know little of how parents and adolescents from immigrant families experience their own internal conflicts in a conflicted situation.

In this chapter, drawing on in-depth student interview data, we address domains of acculturation-based conflict, parent and adolescent internal conflicts, and conflict resolution by examining the nuanced experiences of high-achieving Chinese American students attending a highly competitive high school in a cosmopolitan city in the northeastern United States. We focus specifically on high-achieving students because the psychosocial experiences of high-achieving Chinese American students have been overlooked in the past because of the "model minority" stereotype, which implies that Chinese American students are problem-free and well-adjusted high-achievers (Louie, 2004; Qin, 2008). Examining domains, parent and adolescent internal conflicts, and resolution of conflicts in families with high-achieving Chinese American students can help researchers glean important information about the specific vulnerabilities among this group of students. In the current chapter, we focus specifically on *students' perceptions of conflicts with parents* in these families.

Conflict and Resolution in Traditional Chinese Families

Traditional Chinese families are governed by Confucianism, which constitutes the fundamental base of philosophy in East Asia that defines one's self-worth, ethics of family relations, and social norms (Ho et al., 1991). Confucian values encourage individuals to de-stress the uniqueness of their personal achievement, intentions, or objectives to develop a *relational* self, who lives for "the sake of the others" (*wei-jen*; Tu, 1976, p. 114). Accordingly, child development from a Chinese cultural perspective is better described as a process of learning to forgo personal needs and desires to satisfy parental and societal expectations and maintain interdependence in the social network (Ho et al., 1991; Lam, 1997). In Yang's (1986) review on traditional Chinese parenting, parents socialize children to be filial through cultivating obedience, self-constraint, dependency, and modesty early on in their development. In intergenerational communication, Chinese parents, as authority figures, are assigned the power to decide almost everything for their children, out of fear that children's erroneous decisions may lead to a loss of face or loss in financial interests for the whole family (Cooper, 1999; Hwang, 2000; Lam, 1997). Children are expected to show respect, suppress their anger or discontent, and sacrifice personal goals to satisfy parental expectations (Chao & Tseng, 2002; Yang, 1986).

When conflicts do arise, how do children negotiate their incompatible stances with their parents? In Hwang's (2000) review on Chinese relationalism, he delineated three categories of social relations: (1) the vertical in-group, (2) the horizontal in-group, and (3) the horizontal out-group. In the vertical in-group, a person with subordinate status faces a conflict with a person of superior status in the same social group. The subordinate's priority is to tend to the superior's "face" and to maintain a harmonious relationship through choosing endurance and indirect communication as responses. In a horizontal in-group conflict situation, two individuals have equal status, but with the same priority of maintaining interpersonal harmony, which allows each individual to adopt more direct communication styles, often utilizing compromise as the means to resolve conflict. Finally, in a horizontal out-group, two individuals belong to different groups and have equal status and one can openly strive for personal objectives, even at the cost of severing the relationship. According to this model, Chinese parent–child conflict management is predominantly governed by the vertical in-group relationship. When in conflict with their parents, children should protect parents' face unconditionally, avoid direct expressions of personal needs, and obey parental decisions. It is possible for this vertical in-group relationship to shift toward a more horizontal pattern if parents are willing to forgo some part of their authority. In this latter situation, children may be able to assert their voices and needs more. However, they still need to save their parents' face and strive for a compromise with their parents. In the traditional Chinese family system, the horizontal out-group relationship does not usually apply (Hwang, 2000).

Conflicts and Communication: A Focus on Chinese American Families

What happens to Chinese families after they have immigrated to the United States? Do cultural emphases on harmony and obedience continue to suppress conflicts, or do immigration and acculturation gaps between parents and children disturb family equilibrium and evoke new conflicts and resolution styles? And are immigrant parents and their adolescents indeed so polarized in their values and beliefs after migration?

Domains of Conflicts. In the literature, Chinese American families have sometimes been portrayed as "tightly knit," relatively conflict free and highly cohesive (Ho, 1998; Tan, 2004; Uba, 1994). The underlying assumption is that parents and children continue to suppress conflicts due to cultural norms (Tan, 2004). However, research shows that immigration-related factors such as an acculturation gap between parents and children—children picking up English and absorbing the U.S. culture faster and more strongly than their foreign-born parents—often disrupts family relations and contributes to elevated levels of conflicts (Crane, Ngai, Larson, & Hafen, 2005; Farver, Narang, & Bhadha, 2002; Qin, 2006). In their chapter, Juang and colleagues (this volume) distinguish acculturation-based conflicts that are relevant for immigrant families undergoing the acculturation process, conflicts rooted in differences over particular cultural values, attitudes, and beliefs, from everyday conflicts that are relevant for all families, i.e., everyday issues that are based on conventional (familial or societal) ways of doing things such as homework, doing household chores, and what to wear. Their findings show that acculturation-based conflicts weaken the quality of parenting and family relations, which in turn contribute to poor adolescent well-being. Their findings also underscore the importance of examining and understanding additional domains of acculturation-based conflicts.

In Juang et al.'s chapter, acculturation-based conflicts (using the Lee et al., 2000, measure) include the following domains: academic expectations, decision-making, and parental expression of love and respect. The domains in Lee and colleagues' scale were based on ethnographic reports (e.g., Sung, 1985) and summaries of research studies (e.g., Uba, 1994) reporting common conflicts resulting from cultural differences between Asian (including Chinese) immigrant parents and their children. These domains were further reviewed and expanded upon by focus groups consisting of Asian American students and Asian American mental health experts who were asked to "identify and describe additional typical family conflicts that they believed were attributable in part to acculturation differences between parents and children" (Lee et al., 2000, p. 212). Previous studies using quantitative methods have identified a few other domains of acculturation-related conflicts in Chinese American families: career choice, language barriers, and limited time to communicate (Costigan & Dokis, 2006; Hwang, Wood, & Fujimoto, 2010; Okubo et al., 2007). However, quantitative standardized surveys used in these studies are limited by their reliance on previously established areas. Quantitative methods are also limited in their capacities to uncover how different domains of acculturation-based conflicts interact with each other and escalate conflicts between immigrant parents and their adolescent children. Therefore, more qualitative research is sorely needed to capture additional domains as well as the unique interactive complexities of acculturation-based conflicts in Chinese American families.

Parent and Adolescent Internal Conflicts. In the conception of acculturation-based conflicts in immigrant families, the assumption is often that children, having grown up in the U.S., are more influenced by the U.S. culture and crave more autonomy and independence especially as they reach adolescence. Parents, on the other hand, want more interdependence and control (Juang et al., this volume; Kwak, 2003; Qin, 2008). Based on self-perceptions of adolescents and college students, a large body of research highlights that Chinese American parents tend to restrict youths' autonomy in decision-making, self-assertion in communication, and self-realization in their educational or career pursuits (e.g., Cooper, 1999; Leong, Kao, & Lee, 2004; Okubo et al., 2007; Russell, Crockett, & Chao, 2010). Chinese American youth, on the other hand, are fast in absorbing the U.S. culture and desire autonomy and independence-oriented parent–child relationships. Indeed, parents and children develop different but *parallel* dual frames of reference: Parents tend to compare their children's behaviors with those of children in China or their own experiences and want their children to be more obedient, whereas immigrant children tend to compare their experiences with those of their friends or what they see depicted in U.S. media and hope their parents can give them more independence (Qin, 2006). Having dissonant views on the autonomy versus connectedness issue has been indicated as a major source amplifying family conflict and hampering Chinese American youths' psychological adjustment (Hwang et al., 2010; Juang, Syed, & Takagi, 2007). The earlier-mentioned line of research places parent–child dynamics squarely in the independent-collective model (Markus & Kitayama, 1991) that has dominated discussions on Asian and West cultures. Are parents and children indeed so rigid and polarized in their cultural orientations when they interact with each other in a conflicted situation? Again, quantitative methods are limited in their capacity to uncover the nuanced experiences and internal conflicts parents and children may experience in a particular situation. In this chapter, drawing on student interview data, we report youths' perceptions of internal conflicts experienced by both themselves and their immigrant parents in their daily dynamic interactions.

Conflict Resolution Styles. Research suggests that conflict resolution approaches can be "constructive" or "destructive" (Montemayor, 1986). Constructive resolution occurs as a result of competent approaches in communication including initiating problem solving, emphasizing commonalities, accepting responsibility, and showing empathy. Destructive resolution occurs due to incompetent approaches including demanding unilateral behavior or adopting avoidance strategies (Comstock, 1994). Conflict-resolution styles are also associated with family and child outcomes. For example, findings indicated that constructive, authoritative conflict schema (compliance as a result of mutual respect) occurred more often among well-adjusted adolescents in families with higher levels of cohesion, whereas less-constructive approaches (e.g., authoritarian and indulgent conflict schemas) were particularly associated with low levels of psychosocial adjustment in adolescents and low levels of cohesion in the family (Jutengren & Palmerus, 2007; Schrodt, 2005).

Most of the previously-mentioned studies on conflict resolution have been conducted on European American families. In Chinese American families, some studies found that by and large, parents and children maintain substantial traditional values in parent–child interactions, especially in conflict resolution. More specifically, to maintain harmony and hierarchical structure at home, Chinese American children are less likely to challenge parental views in public and more likely to obey parental expectations, largely reflecting Hwang's vertical in-group resolution style (e.g., Lee et al.,

2005; Okubo et al., 2007). However, a number of other studies suggest that, influenced by American values, many immigrant parents adjust their mode of communication and conflict management and adopt more democratic approaches and respect of the autonomy of children, reflecting more the horizontal in-group resolution style (e.g., Kwak, 2003; Qin, 2008). Although one may expect differences in samples to partially explain the differences found in conflict-resolution styles used (for example, Qin's 2008 sample consisted largely of adolescents of recently arrived immigrant parents, whereas Lee et al.'s 2005 sample consisted of college students with parents from diverse backgrounds in generational status and length of time in the United States), it is not entirely clear how immigrant parents with varied length of time in the United States and their high-achieving adolescents may resolve their conflicts.

Our review of research on conflicts in Chinese American families shows that existing studies, largely quantitative, are inadequate in uncovering additional domains of acculturation-based conflicts, exploring parent and adolescent internal conflicts, and in addressing conflicted resolution styles, especially in families with high-achieving students. To fill these gaps in the literature, the current study had three primary goals: (1) to analyze in-depth student interview data to identify additional domains of acculturation-based conflicts in families with high-achieving Chinese American students from a highly competitive high school in the northeastern region of the United States, (2) to examine internal conflicts parents and their high-achieving adolescents may experience in conflicted situations, and (3) to investigate the approaches most commonly used for conflict resolution in these families.

Method

The current study reports on qualitative interview data collected with students as part of a larger project designed to understand the psychosocial development of high-achieving students, with a specific focus on Asian American students. Participants were recruited from a highly selective public high school located in a northeastern metropolis of the United States. The school was one of three public high schools run by the city's Board of Education to serve the needs of academically gifted students. The school was chosen because over 60% of the student population was Asian American. Students were admitted based solely on the Specialized High School Admission Test (Krane, 2001); less than 5% of students who take the test are eventually admitted into the school. The entire cohort of ninth graders was invited to participate in a survey ($N = 825$). Students were told that the study focused on the schooling experiences and mental health of high-achieving students. Parental consent was obtained from 745 students who participated in the study. The sample for the current study consisted of 18 students selected to participate in in-depth interviews to further understand the students' experiences at home and school and how these experiences may be related to their mental health. Thus, the subsample was selected based on their composite mental health score as measured by depression (Children's Depression Inventory; Kovacs, 1985), anxiety (Revised Children's Manifest Anxiety Inventory; Reynolds & Richmond, 1978), and self-esteem (Rosenberg, 1965). Students were all Chinese American, chosen randomly from the first quartile, last quartile, and 50th percentile of the composite mental health value. In the current sample, 7 (39%) were boys and 11 (61%) were girls. Adolescents were 16 or 17 years old ($M = 16.56$ years). A majority was U.S.-born ($n = 14$, 78%), and four participants (22%) were born in Chinese communities (i.e., three in China, one in Macau). Nine fathers (50%) were engaged in service-type jobs (e.g., a chef in a restaurant or a plumber), two worked as professionals (11%), three were self-employed (17%), and four fathers' careers (22%) were unknown. Among mothers, seven (39%) were employed (four service-type jobs, three professionals), two were self-employed (11%), and four were unemployed (22%); five mothers' careers (28%) were unknown. All participants came from two-parent families.

All student interviews were conducted in English and transcribed verbatim (all the names used in this chapter are pseudonyms). The semi-structured interview was guided by a protocol that included a list of questions on parent–child relations, parent–child conflicts, parent–child communication, students' mental health, and schooling experiences. The interview lasted 1–2 hours. Interviews were conducted by the first author or a trained research assistant. Both spent substantial time at the school doing fieldwork prior to the interviews. Data analysis was guided by a grounded-theory approach and involved initially reading through transcripts and writing memos. Next, data were uploaded onto Atlas-Ti, a computer-aided qualitative research software (Atlas-Ti 5.0). Three authors conducted the data analysis. We first did open coding (Strauss & Corbin, 1990). The purpose of coding is to fracture (Strauss & Corbin, 1990) the data to rearrange it into categories that facilitate the comparison of data within and between these categories and that aid in the development of theoretical concepts (Maxwell, 1996). The codes were developed inductively from existing theories as well as by the researchers during the analysis (e.g., "Conflicts on Grades," "Parental Repetition on Grades," and "Avoiding Conflict Resolution"; Maxwell, 1996). Next, axial coding was conducted, which involves grouping the codes and concepts into higher-level conceptual categories (Strauss & Corbin, 1990). For example, codes such as Parental Repetition on Grades, Parental Comparison, and Yelling for Bad Grades were grouped into the category of Process of Conflict: Educational Expectations. Finally, in selective coding, we integrated the categories that were developed in our data analyses to form the initial theoretical framework. To monitor researcher bias and check for reliability of the codes and categories, the three researchers who coded the data met three times. Codes and categories were crosschecked, and discrepancies were discussed and used to refine the categories.

Findings

Our findings indicate that the adolescents in our study struggled with many of the everyday conflicts found in previous research on Chinese American adolescents, such as routines, friends, privacy, appearance, and computer use (see Juang et al., this volume). Our in-depth examination, however, revealed four main domains of acculturation-based conflicts (i.e., parental educational pressure, especially in how this was communicated; attitudes toward other races; feelings toward parent country of origin and identity; and cultural and language barriers). We consider these conflicts acculturation-based conflicts because our analyses demonstrate that each of these four conflict domains was rooted in parent and adolescent differences in values, attitudes, and beliefs as a result of them growing up and being socialized in different cultures and parental immigration experiences. Together, these domains interact with each other in escalating conflicts in these families with high-achieving adolescents. Furthermore, our analyses of student interview data suggest that both parents and adolescents experienced some internal conflicts in their dynamic relations. Finally, our findings show that adolescents perceived resolution of such conflict to follow more of a vertical in-group model in their families. We illustrate and elaborate upon these ideas below.

Conflicts Related to Educational Pressure. Given that all of our participants had been admitted into one of the most competitive and high-achieving schools in the country, we expected education to be less of an issue of contention at home for these adolescents. However, our findings demonstrated that education-related issues remained the most common domain of conflicts in the students' families. Our analyses showed that conflicts did not arise simply because of high parental expectations. In many ways, the students in our sample had deeply internalized high parental expectations and were intrinsically motivated to do well academically. In most families, conflicts occurred because of how these expectations were communicated. In data analysis, we found three themes around parental communication around education-related issues that often caused the most conflicts: parental repetition, parental emotional reactions to their occasional failures in school, and parents' constant comparison of them with students who had even higher levels of achievement.

Repetitions. In more than half of the families, students talked about education being a "family matter," causing frequent friction and tension at home. This was the case in Susan's home. For her, she often did not want to talk about school because "I already have enough of it [at school]." Nevertheless, her mother wanted to talk about it more:

Some dinners are really like bad because she just talks sometimes and if I disagree with her, then we just start this whole argument. She's like, "Oh, you have to do good on your SATs . . . you have to work on your essays.". . . They just repeatedly talk about school. They would start saying something about school, and then, I would say something, and they would say something, and eventually I would touch upon a point that they don't want me to say, and then it will get into this whole big thing. . . . It's kind of the norm.

For Susan, her parents' over focus on education was annoying to her. During the interviews, many students expressed a similar resentment toward their parents' repetitions. For example, Vincent shared his feelings: "I'm trying to live up to their standards. But sometimes it gets tiresome having them reiterate everything." Similarly, Ming complained about his parents, "[when I get a bad grade] . . . they start yelling, they give me these really long talks and lectures . . . I guess like, as they're getting older and like so, they're getting like, they're getting like really forgetful, so I guess they forgot they already told me about how important college was and then like, so yeah it's basically every week."

From the students' perspective, because of their parents' experience of immigration, they offered "that extra push." Sometimes students like Lucy interpreted their parents' high expectation as a means to achieve their own unrealized American Dream: "I think it's kind of like part of American Dream kind of thing because people obviously immigrate to America for better opportunities . . . and they themselves have almost no chance of actually becoming doctors or lawyers, but they want their children to maybe live out their dreams."

Reactions to "failures." Another area of conflict around education reported by students was that their parents often had very strong emotional reactions to their "failures" in school, including getting angry and yelling. This was related to the strong parental emphasis on educational outcomes partially resulting from their own immigration status. For example, in Angela's family, she described her mother's strong reaction, "Yeah, my mom worries. She pretends not to, but then when I fail, she really has a heart attack." Similarly, Alex wished her parents would lighten up a bit, "They just take everything so literally, and exaggerate, like if I get one bad grade, they think, 'Oh no, you're going to fail school, you're going to become one of those bad girls who do drugs' and things like that." Often, from the students' perspectives, parents were "paranoid" and they attributed this paranoia to their parents' immigrant background. Specifically, because their parents had to give up everything and start a new life in the United States, they lacked a sense of security and well-established network of support in the new society. As a result, youths felt that parents pushed their children extra hard to compensate for the potential disadvantages associated with being an immigrant. Students also believed that parents hoped their children could realize their own dreams of success in the new land.

Students felt that their Chinese parents often considered their failure as a personal assault that shamed the whole family. This reaction often triggered feelings of guilt and self-blame in students who were very sensitive to parental reactions. For example, Peter talked about how his mother's reaction made him feel bad:

> Main conflicts around . . . the way she gets really angry like at a failing grade . . . I don't know what I'm afraid of, but whenever I get a bad grade, I just feel so bad about it. And I wouldn't tell my mom sometimes. And like if she finds out, she just like yells at me, and asks me why I did that. And that I should take off my work and everything.

Parental comparisons. Another common source of conflicts was parents' comparisons of their children with others who were academically superior to them as a way of motivating their children. During interviews students commented that for their parents, this is an often-used strategy to motivate them to study harder to succeed. For students who grew up in the United States, however, they resented not being judged for their own worth and value. In these parental comparisons, the reference group could be inside the family or outside the family, for example, someone in the newspaper, other students at the school, parents' friends' children, siblings, or relatives. Their children attending such a competitive school sometimes provided parents more reasons to compare. For example, Lucy said during the interview,

> And the school, all the parents know each other somehow. And when something happens, all of a sudden, all the parents are like, "Oh my god, that girl got into Harvard. Did you hear? Oh my god, she got into Harvard." And then they turn around and they face you and they're like, "Oh, did you see that girl?" And they sort of like set this kind of goal for you, but it's like their own kind of image.

Students complained bitterly about such comparisons during the interview. For example, Ming said his parents often told him "Oh blah blah blah is like doing so much better." and "I really hate it when they compare me to other people, but like, like that feels really low to me."

Students also reported that their parents frequently compared them to their siblings or cousins and used their superior achievement to motivate their child. In Ming's family, a constant reference was his older sister who also graduated from the same high school and was now attending an Ivy League university. Ming's parents hoped that he could follow in his sister's footsteps: "Like she is the one that is like excelling in everything . . . She's interning for the Department of Justice. She's doing like all this really high-end-like high-achieving things . . . and then I feel like I have to live up to my sister's standards. Or else I'd be kind of like a failure." Students noted that their parents often used this kind of comparison to motivate them to perform better. However, it often had the opposite effect. For Ming, the effect of his parents' constant comparison and pressure was unbearable and had a very negative influence on his mental health, "it's just like you can't feel like you can function and like yeah, usually after my parents lecture me, I feel like I, like usually, the least that affected me would be like low self-esteem, but the worst would be like, like real depression. Like the kind that you can't function anymore."

Conflicts Related to Other Races. Besides educational pressure, another salient theme in the interviews involved value conflicts students had with their parents in daily life. Their conflicted values were most clearly discernible through what children or parents considered as offensive in each other's behaviors or verbal expressions, which was rooted in their cultural differences in values and beliefs. According to students' narratives, Chinese immigrant parents often found children's disrespectful behaviors or expressions offensive. Children, on the other hand, were most often offended by their parents' "racist" remarks and attitudes toward people from other ethnic groups, especially those of African American, Latino, or Japanese descent. For example, Lijuan, whose parents both came from Guangdong, China, said she often argued with her mother about attitudes toward other races:

> My mom kind of discriminates a lot . . . like she has this discrimination about Blacks and Mexicans . . . she sees a Black guy and she'll be like, "Oh, he's not good at study, he must be great at sports." And I'm like, "You don't have any basis for that. You don't even know him. You can't do that to him.". . . I don't know how she can make judgment on people like that. I hate that. I argue with her everyday about that pretty much.

Another student, Elizabeth, talked about similar contentions she had with her father:

> I was just talking to my sister. He sort of just stepped into the conversation, and like he said, "Oh, all Black people, not all, but you know Black people, they're not really. . ." And like, I sort of just left the house after that. And my mom came after me and she told me that like, because everyone in our family has been mugged by like Black people at least once. So yeah, he has a reason to not like them . . . but I'm the exact opposite, which is why we always fight a lot.

In many ways, conflicts Chinese immigrant parents and their children experienced around race reflect their parallel dual frames of references (Qin, 2006). The students in our study, nearly all born in the United

States, grew up in a very cosmopolitan, multiracial city. They were likely to have had a lot of exposure to people of different ethnic backgrounds and thus may have developed a more open mind toward differences. Their parents, on the other hand, nearly all born abroad, were mostly socialized in their countries of origin where they might have formed certain ideas of other races based on the media or other indirect sources. For parents such as Elizabeth's who lived in urban areas with other ethnic minorities, occasional negative interactions were unavoidable. Parents tended to translate these experiences into racist attitudes against the particular ethnic minority group. Children, however, reported that they were less likely to attribute isolated negative incidents to the whole group—as Elizabeth said, she was the "exact opposite." They were more likely to see the differences within a group. For example, Thomas commented on his feelings about race that were different from his mother's "I mean, she's been around much longer than I have . . . But so far, what I've experienced, everyone is different." Students often used strong words of dissent in discussing their feelings about parental racist remarks. For example, Thomas commented on his father's racist attitudes, "I hate some of his discriminations."

Conflicts Related to Country of Origin and Identity. Another area of conflict between parents and children were feelings toward the parents' country of origin. About two-thirds of the students interviewed said they were proud to be "Chinese." However, growing up in the United States, children were also exposed to more ambivalent impressions of their parents' country of origin. Sometimes in conversations, children would express their mixed feelings to their parents. They indicated during the interviews that this could be upsetting to their parents. For example, Elizabeth talked about her "pride" in being Chinese, "because China has such like an awesome culture." However, she also acknowledged that, "I'm not a big fan of the Communist thing." Similarly, in Lijuan's home, her mother "preached having pride in the Chinese culture" a lot. However, there were things about China that she did not feel proud of. When she shared those with her mother, her mother would say, "What are you talking about? We're great." She admitted that sometimes she made hurtful statements against China, which caused her mother to become upset.

A few students talked about their parents sometimes forcing them to choose between China and the United States. For example, Adam commented on his parents: "they've asked me like five times, 'like if something were to happen between like America and China, which one would you like?' I hate when they do that because it's just really unfair. Like why would I have to choose?" Oftentimes, Adam just refused to answer: "I would change the topic or something like that because I don't really want to answer."

Conflicts Related to Cultural and Language Barriers. Another area of acculturation-based conflict students discussed during the interviews was cultural misunderstandings and language barriers. Many of the cultural misunderstandings were rooted in parents' lack of knowledge of common practices and adolescents' lived realities. For example, in Elizabeth's home, she wanted to dye her hair like some of her peers at school. However, her mother was strongly against her doing so because she worried that dying her hair might cause brain cancer.

In data analysis, we also found that language barriers compromised parent–child communication, creating more chances for misunderstanding and conflicts during communication. Nearly all families experienced a language barrier to some degree. Often, children's native language ability was lost over time and they spoke English with much more proficiency. For parents, it was often the opposite. As a result, communication became highly unpredictable at home, causing a lot of frustration and potential conflicts as a result of misunderstanding. For children, not being able to express their thoughts and feelings was very frustrating. For example, Alex talked about her frustration, "I'm not really that good with Chinese. And sometimes I have to use Chinglish—a little bit of Chinese and English. And they go like, 'What?' And I get frustrated, and I say, 'Forget it.' . . . Makes me feel really frustrated that I can't explain something."

The language barriers created misunderstandings, which then became a catalyst for conflicts. This misunderstanding happened quite often in Tiffany's family: "I speak English, and my mom speaks to me in Cantonese . . . sometimes, she misunderstands English and she always says like when I say, 'Liberal Arts,' in school. She's like 'Arts, you want to go into Art?'" In this case, the mother misunderstood "Liberal Arts" as "Art" and questioned her daughter's choice. Similar things happened in Max's family, although for him, it was even more frustrating:

> There are times I guess when it gets quote on quote too complicated . . . sometimes, I'll be like, 'Oh, I said the wrong thing, or I expressed my feelings in the wrong way' . . . They egregiously misunderstand me, then I try to explain again. And you know, it's because of the heat of the moment, that they probably aren't even comprehending each other. We're just going at the argument.

In Max's family, misunderstandings exacerbated their heated arguments, making it impossible to ever clarify the misunderstanding while simultaneously creating more misunderstanding with each interchange.

Parents' and Children's Internal Conflicts. In addition to outward conflicts between parents and adolescents, adolescents reported that they themselves, as well as their parents, struggled with internal conflicts.

Conflicted tiger mothers/fathers. In the literature, Chinese American parents are often depicted as singularly focusing on educational achievement at all costs, with some resemblance to the "tiger mother" Amy Chua depicted in her book (Louie, 2004; Sue & Okazaki, 1990). From the students' perspectives, however, parents experienced much more internal conflicts in pushing their children to succeed. They were often torn and internally conflicted about what they wanted for their children. From the students' accounts, when their parents saw that they were under too much pressure and were working too hard (a school survey shows that students in the school on average slept for 5 hours a night), they often felt guilty and empathic and tried to lessen or completely remove the pressure. For example, in Ming's family, his parents exerted a tremendous amount of pressure on him, including threatening to not fund him if he did not get into an Ivy League university. However, at other times, "both my mom and dad are having like kind of this sad-like tone, like 'It's okay, it doesn't really matter. Just try your best.' They don't really like push me to do anything." Similarly, in Lucy's home, her parents asked her if she wanted to "transfer to an alternative less competitive school": "When they [parents] see you working so hard, and you're so tired all the time, they kind of feel guilty for putting you through it . . . They're just like, 'whatever, do your own thing. I don't care anymore if you do well or not. Because it's your life, I don't care. It's too stressful for us'." Likewise, in Vincent's family, his parents who usually pushed him very hard felt sympathetic after seeing their son struggling with his workload, "Because when they see me do all this work, they say, 'Oh my, you're so stressed out. You should relax.' They have all this guilt, like no, they have all this like sympathy for me." Thus, from the students' perspectives, while the parents often tried to control their children and impose high academic standards and expectations on them, they also tried to give their children more autonomy and independence. Endeavors to control their children seemed to engender a lot of stress for both parents and children. As a result, at times, parents would express their desire to let go of their strict control.

Struggling for independence, yet still yearning for parental guidance. Similar to their parents, children were also torn about their feelings in their interactions with parents. Although they clearly resented high parental pressure and control, as discussed earlier, they also felt grateful for parental pressure and craved parental attention in the form of pressure when they felt it was absent. During the interviews, many students talked about feeling "grateful" for their parents' pressure. For example, Max acknowledged that his mother played an important role in his schooling: "If it wasn't for her, I wouldn't be like where I am today." In the absence of parental pressure, they often felt lost and sad. Ming commented on his parents' change of attitude of not pushing him hard at times, "It's like a really huge burden off my chest. I don't have to like really think about it. I feel like I have a lot more options on my table. But then, I myself feel at times kind of sad because I feel like I should be pushed, like someone is supposed to like push me. Because I'm so used to them like encouraging me to do this or do that." Thus, while he resented parental pressure, Ming also felt sad when his parents were not pushing him.

About half of the students in our study came from low socioeconomic families where parents did not receive high levels of education themselves and were quite removed from their children's education. In these families, parents tended to give their children more freedom, letting them be in charge of their education more so than in other families. Although children enjoyed this sense of independence and control, they also wished that their parents would be more involved. For example, Lucas commented on his torn feelings about his parents:

> Like when you don't have parents to help you sometimes, like, push you sort of, you feel like there's something missing . . . sometimes I like enjoy like the relatively larger independence that I have compared to my friends, but then like sometimes like I get back tests and see that they're lower than what I wanted them to be, I sort of wish my parents were there to push me harder sometimes.

For Lucas, while he enjoyed the freedom and independence, he also wished that his parents were not so "detached" from his academic life. Students like Lucas both enjoyed the autonomy and independence they have in their lives *and* yearned for higher expectations and more involvement from their parents. In these families, educational pressure became both a source of contention and a form of parental attention and love.

Internal conflicts around identities. Although parents and children experience conflicts in their attitudes toward other races and feelings toward parent country of origin, analyses of student accounts show that both parents and children seem to have internal conflicts in their own ethnic identities. From the students' perspectives, their parents were often torn about their own ethnic identity and feelings toward China. On the one hand, they wanted to pass on their heritage culture to their children. Many students reported that their parents pushed them to befriend other Asian students as an attempt to keep their heritage culture. However, most parents came to the United States many years ago and have assimilated into the U.S. society. For example, Lucas talked about how his parents moved the whole family closer to Chinatown so that they could be closer to their culture of origin. However, he also commented on his parents' limited knowledge of traditional Chinese customs, "Yeah, like the most they know about is, 'Oh, I get red envelopes on Chinese New Year' stuff like that and like they don't really like know a lot of other aspects of it, like the more traditional stuff." Lucas also talked about his surprise upon discovering his parents' musical tastes:

> It's like it's really surprising when I found out my dad listened to Elvis and Frank Sinatra . . . I found out my mother listened to the Rolling Stones and knew who they were. . . . it's like really shocking . . . because you think like your parents are so like, they're more connected to their culture. But you find they like sometimes have conflicts too.

Interestingly, in many families, the 2008 Olympics brought out these internal conflicts in parents. For example, Elizabeth commented that her parents "are torn between cheering for China and America." Lucas's parents also felt torn, but ended up cheering for China—he followed his parents and did so as well.

Students were also torn in their identities. They wanted to feel proud of the Chinese culture and were often irritated by negative comments from peers about China. For example, Lijuan talked about feeling annoyed by peers who "dissed China": "Twinkie, right? They're yellow or black on the outside but they're white inside . . . he will like, he will like diss China, like will just like totally like destroy the Chinese image . . . it's just annoying sometimes because like I was born here. I guess like I have this connection with China." However, students also felt ambivalent and struggled with the Asian identity in the United States, especially the many stereotypes associated with being Asian, such as Asians are "only good at math," "really quiet," they "go home and study all the time," and "have really strict parents." Although they tried to keep certain aspects of their native culture, they also wanted to break the Asian stereotypes. For example, Lucas talked about his efforts to excel in English and shun math and science: "It's sort of like the feeling that, if you do well in English, it's sort of like, whoa, this Asian kid's doing well in English."

Conflict Resolution Styles. Given these conflicts parents and children routinely had at home, how did they resolve these conflicts? Our analysis found that students largely adopted the vertical in-group resolution style in Hwang's model through compliance, avoidance, or ignoring parents privately. In education-related conflicts, children often internalized parental expectations and in most cases complied with parental wishes. For example, Jessica said when she had conflicts with her parents, she tried to "forget about stuff like go to sleep. I listen to music. . . . I guess I'll give in. I mean, I just listen to them. I don't think we ever really resolve the conflict as a family."

Students also used avoidance as a common strategy to resolve conflicts with their parents. For example, Melanie talked about what happened in her family after conflicts:

> Arguments with my mom and me . . . it's not like, "I'm sorry. I'm sorry." It's not like that at all. It's just the next day, everything's fine so the next morning, "what do you want for breakfast?" And then it's all done, you know . . . But like we don't apologize and that's the thing about my family.

Similarly in Julia's home, "We don't really resolve it. We just have an argument that's like pretty short. Then you know, I go to school the next day, I come home and then it's just normal again." For Suzie, avoidance also seemed to be a solution: "Then we just stop talking to each other for awhile. And then, we just go back." Sometimes when parents pressed too hard, students chose to ignore their parents as a means to cope with conflict in order to prevent direct, escalated confrontations. This was the case in Lijuan's family, "Maybe sometimes my mom can be a little strict, but mostly if she is, I think she's being way too strict I ignore her . . . But now I kind of be like, now it's like 'okay, whatever, I know, I know, I know,' and shut her out."

In some cases, students opted for the horizontal in-group model of conflict resolution and openly argued with their parents. From students' accounts, this could be very upsetting for their parents. For example, Lucy talked about her experiences with her mother,

> I talk back to my mom a lot, and she gets really mad at me. Because she's like, "you should respect your parents." But then, like I guess growing up in America, the teachers are always like, "Oh, voice your opinion. Like speak up for yourself" . . . So then when you do, it's wrong. But if you don't, you're going against everything you've ever been taught. . . . Because Americans are just like, "Stand up for yourself. Speak your mind." And Asians are just like, "Don't talk back to your parents. Listen to whatever we say." So it's like so hard to like follow both at the same time.

This occurred in some other families as well. Lucy's remarks clearly illustrated the conflicted messages she received from home and school, indicating the inherent conflicts between the Chinese and U.S. cultures. Although her parents instructed her that respect was most important, her teachers were telling her to speak her mind and be independent. From the students' accounts, their parents often struggled with this conflict resolution model, which then generated more conflicts between parents and adolescents.

Discussion

Overall, our analyses of Chinese American families with high-achieving adolescents show that acculturation-based parent–adolescent conflicts occurred in the domains of educational pressure, value conflicts (e.g., attitudes toward other races and country of origin), and cultural and language barriers. Although students in our sample did have high levels of educational achievement evidenced by admission into this highly competitive school that only enrolled 5% of its applicants, educational pressure remained a salient issue that generated conflicts in most families. In particular, how high expectations were communicated, especially the well-established negative communication patterns, seemed to matter more than the expectations themselves in engendering conflicts. Cultural misunderstanding and language barriers further exacerbated parent–adolescent communication. Our students' accounts also uncover very important internal conflicts both adolescents and parents had along the cultural tightrope of autonomy and relatedness as well as in their ethnic identities.

In conflict resolution, students' strategies (i.e., compliance, avoidance, or ignoring parental advice privately) largely reflect Hwang's (2000) vertical in-group conflict resolution model. A few students reported that they openly argued and talked back to their parents (reflecting the horizontal in-group conflict resolution model), but acknowledged that parents reacted very negatively to this style.

Our study contributes to the current research on conflicts in Chinese American families in the following three ways. First, we have identified two additional domains of acculturation-based conflict in these Chinese American families: attitudes toward other races and feelings toward parents' country of origin. Further, our findings illustrate how these acculturation-based conflicts may interact in generating parent–child conflicts in these families. In particular, communication (e.g., language barriers and negative communication patterns) is a domain of acculturation-based conflict that interacts with and exacerbates other domains of acculturation-based conflicts.

Second, our findings indicate that parent–child conflicts are much more nuanced and complicated than previously depicted. Our students' accounts suggested that both children and parents had internal conflicts. For parents, they wanted to exert high levels of control and push their children toward success, which will bring honor to the family, but at the same time appeared to feel guilty for doing so and tried to give the children more independence and control over their own educational endeavors. Children, on the other hand, wanted more independence, but at the same time felt sad when parental pressure was absent. In previous discussions, parents are often depicted as operating primarily with an Asian cultural emphasis on collectivity, interdependence, and relatedness while children, influenced by the Western U.S. culture, want more autonomy and independence (e.g., Okubo et al., 2007; Russell et al., 2010). However, evidence of parent and adolescent internal conflicts that emerged in our study suggests that relatedness and autonomy co-exist in parent–child dynamics in Chinese American families. In the dynamic cultural model proposed by Tamis-LeMonda and colleagues (2008; also see discussion in Juang et al., this volume), autonomy and relatedness exist in all cultures, but relate to each other in different ways: conflicting (one emphasized over the other), additive (both desirable), and functionally dependent (one is necessary for promoting the other). Our findings demonstrate that instead of parents and children operating on parallel lines, relatedness and autonomy co-exist in *both* parents and children (i.e., reflecting the additive, dynamic nature of these two traditionally polarized traits in parent–child interactions).

Third, our findings show that Hwang's (2000) model fits well with the conflict resolution style of students in our sample. Students reported that they predominantly used compliance, avoidance, or ignoring to resolve conflicts at home, largely reflecting the vertical in-group orientation in

Huang's model. In most of the cases, these conflicts were never resolved. These strategies reflecting more authoritarian or avoiding schemas may be deemed "incompetent" or "destructive" as conflict resolution styles have previously been conceptualized (e.g., Comstock, 1994; Jutengren & Palmerus, 2007). However, it is important to note that there may be cultural differences in what is considered a "constructive" or "destructive" conflict resolution style. Although the vertical in-group resolution model may be considered "destructive" by the typologies developed on European American populations that favor open and direct communication, it fits the Chinese cultural norms and expectations centering on filial piety, face saving, and harmony preservation, and thus may not have so many "destructive" consequences in Chinese American families as in European American families. The horizontal in-group resolution style may be considered "constructive," in Chinese American families like Lucy's; nevertheless, it could actually cause more conflict. Future research should examine the consequences of different conflict resolution styles within a cultural context, with attention to the acculturation process to provide a more nuanced understanding of what constitutes a destructive versus constructive style in families.

Conclusion

Currently in the United States, one out of every five children and adolescents come from families with at least one immigrant parent (Suárez-Orozco, Suárez-Orozco, & Todorova, 2008). Acculturation-based conflicts are likely to occur in many of these families. Using a qualitative approach, our study uncovered additional areas of acculturation-based conflicts not discussed in previous literature, and also demonstrated that parent–child conflict is a dynamic, nuanced process. Importantly, we discovered that *both* parents and adolescents may experience internal conflicts when engaging in conflict. Studies that capture these complexities are important for moving beyond a simplistic picture of immigrant families where conflict is portrayed as polarized, inherent, and inevitable. It is important for future research to draw on different methodological approaches to understand domains of acculturation-based conflicts, parent and child internal conflicts, and resolution styles in immigrant families. The more we understand the mechanisms, lived experiences, and resolution of these conflicts, the better we can help support immigrant family functioning and the healthy development of adolescents from these families.

References

Atlas-Ti 5.0 (2004). *Scientific software development*, Thousand Oaks, CA: Sage.
Chao, R. K., & Tseng, V. (2002). Parenting of Asians. In M. H. Bornstein (Ed.), *Handbook of parenting* (2nd ed., Vol. 4, pp. 59–93). Mahwah, NJ: Erlbaum.

Chua, A. (2011). Why Chinese mothers are superior. *The Wall Street Journal*. Retrieved from http://online.wsj.com/article/SB10001424052748704111504576059713528698754.html.

Comstock, J. (1994). Parent-adolescent conflict: A developmental approach. *Western Journal of Communication, 58*(4), 263–382.

Cooper, C. R. (1999). Multiple selves, multiple worlds: Cultural perspectives on individuality and connectedness in adolescent development. In A. S. Masten (Ed.), *Cultural processes in child development: The Minnesota symposia on child psychology* (Vol. 29, pp. 25–57). Mahwah, NJ: Erlbaum.

Costigan, C. L., & Dokis, D. P. (2006). Relations between parent-child acculturation differences and adjustment within immigrant Chinese families. *Child Development, 77*(5), 1252–1267.

Crane, D. R., Ngai, S. W., Larson, J. H., & Hafen, M., Jr. (2005). The influence of family functioning and parent-adolescent acculturation on North American Chinese adolescent outcomes. *Family Relations, 54*, 400–410.

Farver, J.A.M., Narang, S. K., & Bhadha, B. R. (2002). East meets West: Ethnic identity, acculturation, and conflict in Asian Indian families. *Journal of Family Psychology, 16*(3), 338–350.

Ho, D.Y.F. (1998). Filial piety and filicide in Chinese family relationships: The legend of Shun and other stories. In U. P. Cielen & A. L. Comunian (Eds.), *The family and family therapy in international perspective* (pp. 134–149). Rome, Italy: Edizioni Lint Trieste S. R. L.

Ho, D.Y.F., Chen, S. J., & Chiu, C. Y. (1991). Relational orientation: In search of methodology for Chinese social psychology. In K. S. Yang & K. K. Hwang (Eds.), *Chinese psychology and behavior* (pp. 49–66). Taipei, Taiwan: Laureate. [in Chinese]

Hwang, K. K. (2000). Chinese relationalism: Theoretical construction and methodological considerations. *Journal for the Theory of Social Behaviour, 30*, 155–178.

Hwang, W. C., Wood, J. J., & Fujimoto, K. (2010). Acculturative family distancing (AFD) and depression in Chinese American families. *Journal of Consulting and Clinical Psychology, 78*(5), 655–667.

Juang, L. P., Syed, M., Cookston, J. T., Wang, Y., & Kim, S. Y. (2012). Acculturation-based and everyday family conflict in Chinese American Families. In L. P. Juang & A. J. Umaña-Taylor (Eds.), *Family conflict among Chinese- and Mexican-origin adolescents and their parents in the U.S. New Directions for Child and Adolescent Development, 135*, 13–34.

Juang, L. P., Syed, M., & Takagi, M. (2007). Intergenerational discrepancies of parental control among Chinese American families: Links to family conflict and adolescent depressive symptoms. *Journal of Adolescence, 30*, 965–975.

Jutengren, G., & Palmèrus, K. (2007). The potential role of conflict resolution schemas in adolescent psychosocial adjustment. *Social Indicators Research, 83*, 25–38.

Kovacs, M. (1985). The Children's Depression Inventory (CDI). *Psychopharmacology Bulletin, 21*, 995–999.

Krane, S. (2001). *New York City Specialized Science High Schools Admission Test*. New York, NY: ARC.

Kwak, K. (2003). Adolescents and their parents: A review of intergenerational family relations for immigrant and non-immigrant families. *Human Development, 46*(2–3), 115–136. doi:10.1159/000068581

Lam, C. M. (1997). A cultural perspective on the study of Chinese adolescent development. *Child and Adolescent Social Work Journal, 14*, 95–113.

Lee, R. M., Choe, J., Kim, G., & Ngo, V. (2000). Construction of the Asian American Family Conflicts Scale. *Journal of Counseling Psychology, 47*(2), 211–222.

Lee, R. M., Su, J., & Yoshida, E. (2005). Coping with intergenerational family conflict among Asian American college students. *Journal of Counseling Psychology, 52*(3), 389–399.

Leong, F.T.L., Kao, E.M.-C., & Lee, S.-H. (2004). The relationship between family dynamics and career interests among Chinese Americans and European Americans. *Journal of Career Assessment, 12*, 65–84.

Louie, V. (2004). *Compelled to excel: Immigration, education, and opportunity among Chinese Americans.* Stanford, CA: Stanford University Press.

Markus, H. R., & Kitayama, S. (1991). Culture and the self: Implications for cognition, emotion, and motivation. *Psychological Review, 98*(2), 224–253.

Maxwell, J. (1996). *Qualitative research design.* London, England: Sage Publications.

Montemayor, R. (1986). Family variation in parent-adolescent storm and stress. *Journal of Adolescent Research, 1*(1), 15–31.

Okubo, Y., Yeh, C. J., Lin, P.-Y., Fujita, K., & Shea, J.M-Y. (2007). The career decision-making process of Chinese American youth. *Journal of Counseling and Development, 85*(4), 440–449.

Qin, D. B. (2006). "Our child doesn't talk to us anymore": Alienation in immigrant Chinese families. *Anthropology Education Quarterly, 37*(2), 162–179.

Qin, D. B. (2008). Doing well vs. feeling well: Understanding family dynamics and the psychological adjustment of Chinese immigrant adolescents. *Journal of Youth and Adolescence, 37*(1), 22–35.

Reynolds, C. R., & Richmond, B. O. (1978). What I think and feel: A revised measure of children's manifest anxiety. *Journal of Abnormal Child Psychology, 6*, 271–280.

Rosenberg, M. (1965). *Society and the adolescent self-image.* Princeton, NJ: Princeton University Press.

Russell, S. T., Crockett, L. J., & Chao, R. K. (2010). Introduction. In S. Russell, L. Crockett, & R. Chao (Eds.), *Asian American parenting and parent-adolescent relationships.* New York, NY: Springer Science.

Schrodt, P. (2005). Family communication schemata and the circumplex model of family functioning. *Western Journal of Communication, 69*(4), 359–376.

Strauss, A., & Corbin, J. (1990). *Basics of qualitative research: Grounded theory procedures and techniques.* London, England: Sage Publications.

Suárez-Orozco, C., Suárez-Orozco, M., & Todorova, I., (2008). *Learning a new land: Immigrant students in American society.* Cambridge, MA: Harvard University Press.

Sue, S., & Okazaki, S. (1990). Asian-American educational achievements: A phenomenon in search of an explanation. *American Psychologist, 45*(8), 913–920.

Sung, B. (1985). Bicultural conflicts in Chinese immigrant children. *Journal of Comparative Family Studies, 16*(2). Special issue: Family, kinship and ethnic identity among the Overseas Chinese, 255–269.

Tan, C. B. (2004). *Chinese overseas: Comparative cultural issues.* Hong Kong, China: Hong Kong University Press.

Tu, W. M. (1976). The Confucian perception of adulthood. *Daedalus: Journal of the American Academy of Arts and Science, 105*(2), 109–124.

Uba, L. (1994). *Asian Americans: Personality patterns, identity, and mental health.* New York, NY: Hillsdale Press.

Way, N., & Hamm, J. V. (2005). The experience of close friendship in adolescence. *New Directions for Child and Adolescent Development, No. 107.* NJ: Jossey-Bass.

Wu, C., & Chao, R. K. (2005). Intergenerational cultural conflicts in norms of parental warmth among Chinese American immigrants. *International Journal of Behavioral Development, 29*(6), 516–523.

Yang, K. S. (1986). Chinese personality and its change. In M. H. Bond (Ed.), *The psychology of the Chinese people* (pp. 106–170). New York, NY: Oxford University Press.

Yau, J., & Smetana, J. G. (1996). Adolescent–parent conflict among Chinese adolescents in Hong Kong. *Child Development, 67*, 1262–1275.

DESIREE BAOLIAN QIN *is an assistant professor of human development and family studies at Michigan State University, East Lansing. E-mail: dqin@msu .edu, webpage: http://hdfs.msu.edu/people/faculty/qin-desiree-baolian-edu.*

TZU-FEN CHANG *is a PhD student in the Department of Human Development and Family Studies at Michigan State University, East Lansing. E-mail: changtz@msu.edu*

EUN-JIN HAN *is a PhD student in the Department of Human Development and Family Studies at Michigan State University, East Lansing. E-mail: jinnyhan @msu.edu*

GRACE CHEE *is a PhD student in the Department of Human Development and Family Studies at Michigan State University, East Lansing. E-mail: gracejchee@gmail.com*

Updegraff, K. A., Umaña-Taylor, A. J., Perez-Brena, N. J., & Pflieger, J. (2012). Mother–daughter conflict and adjustment in Mexican-origin families: Exploring the role of family and sociocultural context. In L. P. Juang & A. J. Umaña-Taylor (Eds.), *Family conflict among Chinese- and Mexican-origin adolescents and their parents in the U.S. New Directions for Child and Adolescent Development, 135,* 59–81.

4

Mother–Daughter Conflict and Adjustment in Mexican-Origin Families: Exploring the Role of Family and Sociocultural Context

Kimberly A. Updegraff, Adriana J. Umaña-Taylor, Norma J. Perez-Brena, Jacqueline Pflieger

This study examined the role of mother–daughter conflict in both mothers' and daughters' adjustment. Drawing from ecologically oriented and person–environment fit models, the authors investigated how the family context, as defined by the transition to adolescent motherhood, and the sociocultural context, as measured by mother–daughter discrepancies in cultural orientations, shaped the associations between conflict and adjustment in Mexican-origin families. Overall, conflict was positively related to mothers' and adolescents' depressive symptoms and adolescents' risky behaviors. This relation was strongest when daughters were more Mexican-oriented than their mothers, and weakest when mothers were more Mexican-oriented than their daughters. © 2012 Wiley Periodicals, Inc.

The Supporting MAMI Project was funded by the Department of Health and Human Services (APRPA006011; PI: Umaña-Taylor) and the Cowden Fund to the School of Social and Family Dynamics at Arizona State University. We are grateful to the participants, undergraduate research assistants and interviewers, and the following individuals: Edna Alfaro, Mayra Bamaca, Emily Cansler, Melinda Gonzales-Backen, Amy Guimond, Melissa Herzog, Sarah Killoren, Ethelyn Lara, and Jacqueline Pflieger. The Juntos Project was supported by a grant from NICHD (R01 HD39666; PI: Updegraff) and by the Cowden Fund. We thank the participating families and school districts, and Susan McHale, Ann Crouter, Mark Roosa, Nancy Gonzales, Roger Millsap, Jennifer Kennedy, Melissa Delgado, Lorey Wheeler, Devon Hageman, Lilly Shanahan, Sarah Killoren, Shawna Thayer, and Shawn Whiteman for their assistance in conducting this study.

Conflict with parents is a key process in adolescence, and may be particularly salient in immigrant families as parents and young adolescents are simultaneously negotiating changes in their relationships that may result from the developmental transition through adolescence *and* changes that may result from adapting with another culture. Higher rates of conflict in immigrant as compared with native-born families have been noted in some studies, and a number of scholars have attributed this conflict to intergenerational discrepancies in acculturation, although the evidence is inconsistent (see Birman, 2006, for a review). Existing work suggests that conflict with parents may be an important correlate of adjustment in Mexican-origin families, as conflict between parents and youth has been associated with higher levels of involvement in risk-taking behavior and more frequent symptoms of depression and anxiety (e.g., Lau et al., 2005; Pasch et al., 2006; Updegraff, Delgado, & Wheeler, 2009).

In this chapter, we examine the role of the family and sociocultural context in shaping the associations between mother–daughter conflict and adjustment, drawing from ecologically oriented (Bronfenbrenner & Crouter, 1983; García Coll et al., 1996) and person–environment fit models (Eccles et al., 1993; Lerner & Lerner, 1983). We used data from two unique samples of predominantly immigrant Mexican-origin families to examine the role of family context—a sample of pregnant adolescent girls and their mothers and a same-aged sample of nonpregnant girls and their mothers—to provide an empirical examination of the potential variability introduced into these processes in these two different family contexts. Consistent with the premise of ecological theory that contextual factors interact with one another and with individual characteristics to inform development, we examined whether the context of adolescent pregnancy interacted with adolescent–mother relationship conflict to inform adolescent adjustment. Further, drawing from a person–environment fit model, we considered how the sociocultural context, as defined by discrepancies in mothers' versus daughters' cultural orientations, may exacerbate conflict-adjustment associations in these two family contexts.

Conflict Between Mothers and Daughters

Conflicts between parents and their offspring over daily issues, such as chores, homework, and getting along with sisters and brothers, are viewed as a normative part of adolescence (Laursen & Collins, 2004). As youth seek greater independence and autonomy over their daily lives, parents and youth must renegotiate the rules, expectations, and decision-making processes that govern their relationships. Although most research in this area has focused on European American families, investigations of parent–adolescent conflict processes in ethnic minority samples provide evidence that conflicts over daily issues characterize parent–adolescent relationships in families from a range of cultural backgrounds (e.g., Fuligni, 1998; Smetana & Gaines, 1999).

We focused on conflict between mothers and daughters for several reasons. First, ideas about the gender intensification of socialization pressures in early adolescence (Hill & Lynch, 1983) emphasize the salience of adolescents' relationships with their same-sex parents. From this perspective, mothers assume a significant role in the socialization of their daughters (e.g., Crouter, Manke, & McHale, 1995; Updegraff, McHale, Crouter, & Kupanoff, 2001). Second, some research suggests that conflicts with mothers are more frequent and intense than those with fathers (Scaramella & Conger, 2004), especially conflicts between mothers and daughters (e.g., Laursen, 2005). Because Mexican American families are characterized by an emphasis on traditional gender roles (Cauce & Domenech-Rodríguez, 2002), we expected that conflict between girls and their mothers may be particularly salient for daughters' and their mothers' well-being. Finally, significant associations between conflict with parents and youth adjustment problems have been documented in Latino families (Lau et al., 2005; Pasch et al., 2006; Updegraff et al., 2009), yet we know little about whether and how these associations differ as a function of the characteristics of the family context *within* this culture. Because of the unique circumstances of adolescent motherhood, we examined whether conflict-adjustment linkages differed for Mexican-origin girls experiencing the transition to motherhood versus same-aged Mexican-origin girls who were not transitioning to motherhood.

The Developmental Context of Adolescent Motherhood

Adolescence is a period of significant biological, cognitive, and social transitions. Central to adolescence are the processes of identity formation and autonomy development, when adolescents begin to form a sense of self in multiple domains (Marcia, 1994), to negotiate for greater autonomy and independence (Erikson, 1968), and to develop increasingly realistic plans about their futures (Erikson, 1968; Markus & Wurf, 1987). When pregnancy occurs during adolescence, however, adolescent mothers must *simultaneously* negotiate the normative developmental tasks and the tasks associated with the transition to motherhood. Research on adolescent mothers from different ethnic and racial backgrounds suggests that the challenges of transitioning to motherhood during adolescence place them at risk for maladjustment (Whitman, Borkowski, Keogh, & Weed, 2001). Understanding the implications of adolescent motherhood is particularly important for Mexican-origin female adolescents, as they have the highest birthrate of all ethnic groups in the United States, at over twice the national average (i.e., 94.5 births per 1000; National Vital Statistics Report, 2005).

Mexican American culture is characterized by a strong family orientation, reflected in the emphasis on family members as primary sources of emotional and instrumental support (Cauce & Domenech-Rodríguez, 2002; Marín & Marín, 1991). Within this cultural group, recent immigrant and first-generation families endorse familism values to a greater extent than native-born families (Gonzales et al., 2008). In the context of adolescent pregnancy, young Latina mothers turn to their family members, particularly their own mothers, as primary sources of social support during pregnancy and early years of childrearing (Contreras, Narang, Ikhlas, & Teichman, 2002). In the current chapter, we drew on data from two unique samples to examine whether the typically negative associations between mother–adolescent conflict and adolescent adjustment would be exacerbated in the context of adolescent motherhood (as compared with same-aged adolescents who are not transitioning to motherhood). We anticipated that conflict-adjustment linkages may be stronger for pregnant adolescents compared to nonpregnant adolescents, as daughters may rely on their mothers as primary sources of support during the transition with parenthood, and thus, the salience of conflict for their adjustment may be stronger.

Mother–Daughter Discrepancies in Cultural Orientations

The role of discrepancies between parents and youth in their cultural adaptation has received substantial attention in scholarly writings on immigrant families (Birman, 2006; Portes & Rumbaut, 2001; Szapocznik & Kurtines, 1980; 1993). In work with Cuban American families, Szapocznik and Kurtines (1980, 1993) proposed that problems may arise when youth adapt to U.S. culture at a faster rate than their parents, resulting in strained parent–child relationships, and in turn, youth maladjustment. Discrepancies between parents and adolescents also are possible sources of family and individual adjustment problems from a person–environment fit perspective (Eccles et al., 1993; Lerner & Lerner, 1983). Specifically, from a person–environment fit framework, a mismatch between adolescents' characteristics and the characteristics of their social contexts are expected to be associated with adjustment difficulties. Our focus on discrepancies between mothers' and adolescent daughters' Mexican and Anglo cultural orientations, as an element of the sociocultural context, draws from this perspective and from an ecological model of development, which suggests that individual and environmental characteristics interact to inform development (Bronfenbrenner & Crouter, 1983). As adolescence is a time when youth strive to establish their autonomy and when they become more active in their own cultural development (Umaña-Taylor & Fine, 2004), discrepancies in cultural orientations may be particularly likely to emerge in this developmental period.

The extant literature on intergenerational acculturation gaps suggests that discrepancies that arise when youth acculturate at a faster rate than their parents are the most common or normative type of intergenerational discrepancy (Birman, 2006). Specifically, as youth are involved in settings outside the home (e.g., school, community, peer group) to a greater extent than their parents, they have more opportunities to learn English and become involved in the majority culture while their parents maintain strong ties to the ethnic culture and language. Much less is known about mismatches that are thought to be less common, and thus nonnormative, such as when parents have stronger ties to U.S. culture than youth or when youth maintain stronger ties to Mexican culture than their parents. Some evidence suggests that youths' high levels of involvement in Mexican culture in combination with parents' strong ties to mainstream culture, place youth at risk for adjustment problems (e.g., Updegraff, McHale, Whiteman, Thayer, & Crouter, 2006). In this study, we investigated whether intergenerational discrepancies in Mexican and Anglo cultural orientations exacerbated negative associations between conflict and adjustment. From a person–environment fit perspective, discrepancies that are nonnormative in a particular cultural context (e.g., when mothers are more Anglo-oriented than adolescents or when adolescents are more Mexican-oriented than mothers) may pose more problems for individual adjustment than discrepancies that are normative (Updegraff et al., 2006). Thus, we explored whether cultural discrepancies moderated conflict-adjustment linkages in these two different family contexts (i.e., families experiencing the transition to adolescent motherhood versus not). We focused on depressive symptoms and risky behaviors as indices of adolescent adjustment to assess both internalizing *and* externalizing behaviors, given that previous work has noted that each captures unique aspects of youths' psychosocial functioning and that they are differentially associated with risk factors (Umaña-Taylor & Alfaro, 2009).

An Examination of Mother–Daughter Conflict and Adjustment in Two Family Contexts

In the current chapter, our ecological orientation guides our examination of two family contexts. As a first step, we provide descriptive information regarding conflict, cultural orientations, and adjustment in these two family contexts and then we consider whether the negative associations between conflict and adjustment differed by family context. Next, we present findings illustrating the conditions under which mother–daughter cultural discrepancies moderated the links between conflict and adjustment based on a person–environment fit perspective.

Supporting MAMI Project. Participants of the Supporting MAMI (Mexican-origin Adolescent Mothers and Infants) project were unmarried pregnant Mexican-origin adolescents between 15 and 18 years of age

($N = 207$). Adolescents were invited to participate in the project with a female family member (e.g., mother, aunt, sister) during the final trimester of their pregnancy. In these analyses, we include the 179 adolescents who participated with their biological mothers (87% of the larger sample). Adolescents were an average of 31 weeks' ($SD = 4.51$) pregnant, and an average of 16.21 years of age ($SD = 0.98$), when they participated in the interview. More than half of adolescents were born in the United States (66%) and completed the interview in English (63%). Their mothers averaged 40.40 years of age ($SD = 5.04$) and were most likely to complete the interview in Spanish (69%) and be born in Mexico (67%). Slightly more than one third of mothers (36%) were married to or lived with adolescents' biological fathers. Median household income was $22,000 ($SD = $19,809$).

Juntos ("Together"): Families Raising Successful Teens Project. Participants of the Juntos ("Together"): Families Raising Successful Teens Project (referred to hereafter as the Juntos Project) were 246 adolescents and their mothers recruited as part of a larger study of family and cultural socialization and adolescent development that included mothers, fathers, target adolescents, and older siblings (Updegraff, McHale, Whiteman, Thayer, & Delgado, 2005). For these analyses, 78 adolescent girls who were between 15 and 18 years of age and not pregnant were selected along with their mothers (32% of families in the larger project). Adolescents were 16.03 years of age ($SD = 1.08$), interviewed primarily in English (78%), and were slightly more likely to be born in Mexico (54%) than in the United States (46%). Their mothers averaged 39.08 years of age ($SD = 4.57$), interviewed in Spanish most often (67%), and the majority were born in Mexico (71%). All mothers were married to adolescents' biological fathers (as a result of study criteria). Median household income was $41,000 ($SD = $58,708$).

Procedures and Measures. Adolescents and mothers in both projects participated in individual in-home interviews. Questions were read aloud by bilingual interviewers and recorded on a paper survey for Supporting MAMI participants and a laptop computer for Juntos participants. All participants were interviewed in the language of their choice (i.e., English or Spanish). The same measures were collected in both projects. All materials were translated and back-translated (see Knight, Roosa, & Umaña-Taylor, 2009).

Mothers reported on their annual household incomes, place of birth, and years living in the United States. Adolescents also reported on their country of birth. A log transformation was applied to income to correct for skewness.

Mother–daughter conflict was assessed by asking mothers and adolescents to indicate the frequency of conflict in their relationships during the past year (ranging from $1 = $ *Not at all* to $6 = $ *Several times a day*) regarding daily issues of conflict (e.g., chores, bedtime/curfew, family obligations), using a 10-item scale (Harris, 1992; Smetana, 1988). Sample items are

"How often in the past year have you had disagreements or differences of opinion with your mother about respect for parents such as talking back or being disrespectful?" (adolescent version) and "How often in the past year have you had disagreements or differences of opinion with (adolescent's name) about talking back or being disrespectful?" (mother version). Cronbach's alphas were .79 and .78 for Supporting MAMI and Juntos adolescents, respectively, and .80 for both Supporting MAMI and Juntos mothers.

Adolescents' and mothers' depressive symptoms were measured with the Center for Epidemiological Studies Depression Scale (CES-D; Radloff, 1977). The 20-item measure provides an index of cognitive, affective, and behavioral depressive features (e.g., "I did not feel like eating; my appetite was poor"); adolescents and mothers rated the frequency with which these symptoms had occurred (ranging from 1 = *Rarely or none of the time* to 4 = *Most of the time*) in the past 2 weeks (Supporting MAMI participants) or the past month (Juntos participants). High scores indicated higher levels of depressive symptoms. Cronbach's alphas were .82 for Supporting MAMI adolescents and .89 for Juntos adolescents, and .85 and .88 for Supporting MAMI and Juntos mothers, respectively. Because of the different time periods (i.e., 2 weeks vs. 1 month) used across projects, we standardized depression scores within the project.

Adolescents' reports of risky behaviors were assessed using a measure created by Eccles and Barber (1990), in which adolescents rated their engagement in 24 risky behaviors (e.g., "Gotten drunk or high," "Stayed out all night without your parents' permission") using a 4-point rating scale ranging from *Never* to *More than 10 times* in the past year. Higher scores indicated more risky behavior (αs = .90 and .83, for Supporting MAMI and Juntos adolescents, respectively).

To assess discrepancies in *cultural orientations,* adolescents and their mothers completed the Acculturation Rating Scale for Mexican Americans-II (ARSMA-II; Cuéllar, Arnold & Maldonado, 1995). On a 5-point rating scale, participants indicated how often from 1 (*Not at all*) to 5 (*Extremely often or always*) each of 30 items applied to them during the past year. The Mexican orientation scale included 17 items (e.g., "I like to identify myself as a Mexican American") and the Anglo orientation scale included 13 items (e.g., "I think in English"). For both subscales, Cronbach's alphas were above .85 for Supporting MAMI adolescents and .89 for Juntos adolescents, and above .87 and .88 for Supporting MAMI and Juntos mothers, respectively. To measure discrepancies in Mexican orientations, mothers' Mexican orientation scores were subtracted from adolescents' scores, and similarly, Anglo orientation discrepancies were measured by subtracting mothers' from adolescents' scores. Thus, positive difference scores indicated that adolescents reported higher Mexican or Anglo orientations than mothers, scores near zero indicated that adolescents and mothers reported similar scores, and negative difference scores indicated that mothers reported higher orientations than adolescents.

Mother–Daughter Conflict and Adjustment: Findings from the Supporting MAMI and Juntos Projects

We first provide descriptive information about mother–adolescent conflict, mothers' and adolescents' depressive symptoms, adolescents' risky behaviors, and mothers' and adolescents' Mexican and Anglo orientations in these two unique family contexts (i.e., mother–daughter pairs in the Juntos versus Supporting MAMI samples). Means and standard deviations are found in Table 4.1 and correlations among study variables are found in Table 4.2. Next, we examined the associations between mother–daughter conflict and adolescents' risky behaviors and both adolescents' and mothers' depressive symptoms and tested family context as a moderator of these associations. Finally, we tested whether discrepancies in adolescent–mother Mexican and Anglo cultural orientations moderated conflict-adjustment linkages, and further, whether differences emerged as a

Table 4.1. Means (and Standard Deviations) for Supporting MAMI and Juntos Samples

	MAMI Project (n = 179)		Juntos Project (n = 78)		χ^2
	n	%	n	%	
Family structure (2-parent)	64	36	78	100	90.69***
Nativity (Mexico-born)					
Adolescents	60	34	42	54	9.18***
Mothers	119	67	55	71	
	M	SD	M	SD	$F(1, 255)$
Annual Income (dollars)[a]	27,365	(19,809)	59,883	(58,708)	40.12***
Mother–daughter conflict					
Adolescent reports	2.15	(0.78)	2.53	(0.80)	12.51***
Mother reports	2.32	(0.85)	2.36	(0.79)	
Anglo orientations					
Adolescents	3.68	(0.67)	3.75	(0.84)	
Mothers	2.65	(1.07)	2.83	(0.96)	
Difference score	1.01	(0.98)	0.92	(0.89)	
Mexican orientations					
Adolescents	3.88	(0.71)	3.85	(0.74)	
Mothers	4.07	(0.69)	4.11	(0.67)	
Difference score	−0.15	(0.65)	−0.26	(0.66)	
Depressive symptoms					
Adolescents	1.08	(0.43)	0.97	(0.57)	
Mothers	1.09	(0.49)	0.76	(0.45)	25.01***
Adolescent risky behaviors	1.52	(0.41)	1.42	(0.31)	4.27*

Note: χ^2 difference and F-test values were only included for significant differences.
[a]Degrees of freedom are 1, 237.
*$p < .05$. **$p < .01$. ***$p < .001$.

Table 4.2. Bivariate Correlations Among Study Variables for Supporting MAMI Project (Above the Diagonal) and Juntos Project (Below the Diagonal)

	1.	2.	3.	4.	5.	6.	7.	8.	9.	10.	11.	12.	13.	14.
Income (log)	—	-.09	.22**	-.02	-.01	.24***	.16*	-.02	-.23**	-.13	-.06	-.01	-.29***	.09
Adolescent Nativity	-.55***	—	.11	-.07	-.07	-.41***	-.47***	.24***	.49***	.30***	.18*	-.06	.04	.23***
Family Structure	—	—	—	.03	-.08	-.06	-.17*	.15*	.10	.10	-.02	-.04	-.12	.05
Conflict (adolescent report)	.16	-.15	—	—	.31***	-.03	-.01	-.01	-.02	.03	-.07	.21**	.11	.43***
Conflict (mother report)	.04	.07	—	.12	—	.12	.08	.00	.00	-.07	.04	.19**	.19**	.31***
Adolescent Anglo orientation	.59***	-.58***	—	.21	-.11	—	.44***	.20**	-.39***	-.27***	-.10	.05	-.03	.12
Mother Anglo orientation	.47***	-.65***	—	.13	-.04	.51***	—	-.79***	-.64***	-.64***	.01	.04	-.08	.15
M-A Anglo difference score	.05	.16	—	.06	-.06	.39***	-.59***	—	.44***	.51***	-.09	-.01	.07	-.09
Adolescent Mexican orientation	-.39***	.60***	—	-.21	-.15	-.50***	-.67***	.24*	—	.56***	.45***	.04	.15*	-.17*
Mother Mexican orientation	-.14	.37***	—	-.05	-.05	-.24*	-.46***	.26*	.56***	—	-.48***	-.06	.04	-.11
M-A Mexican difference score	-.28**	.29**	—	-.18	-.12	-.31**	-.28**	.01	.54***	-.39***	—	.09	.12	-.04
Adolescent depressive symptoms	-.10	-.05	—	.14	.09	-.07	.07	-.15	-.15	-.28**	.12	—	.14	.40***
Mother depressive symptoms	-.28*	.35**	—	-.19	.25*	-.13	-.43***	.34***	.30**	.15	.18	.16	—	.16*
Adolescent risky behavior	.09	-.10	—	.42***	.33***	.16	.17	-.04	-.26*	-.32***	.03	.41***	.07	—

Note: Family structure (0 = other; 1 = 2-parent) was a constant for Juntos sample, as all families belonged to two-parent households. M-A = Mother–adolescent. Adolescent nativity coded as 0 = US, 1 = Mexico.
*p < .05. **p < .01. ***p < .001.

function of family context. We calculated Cohen's d to measure effect sizes for our descriptive findings; $d = .20$ is a small effect, $d = .50$ is a moderate effect, and $d = .80$ is a large effect (Cohen, 1988).

Descriptive Findings. In general, adolescent girls and mothers in both samples described levels of conflict below the midpoint on a 6-point scale, suggesting that conflicts occurred slightly less than "a few times each month." Adolescent girls in the Juntos Project reported significantly more conflicts with their mothers than did girls in the Supporting MAMI project over the daily conflict issues measured in this study, $d = .48$, but mothers in the two samples did not differ in their reports of conflict frequency.

To better understand the sources of conflict in these two family contexts, we examined whether there were differences in the frequency of disagreements in each of the ten domains of conflict (see Table 4.3). For several conflict issues, we found that girls in the Juntos project reported more frequent conflicts than did girls in the Supporting MAMI project, with effect sizes ranging from small to moderate. Girls in the Juntos project were more likely to have disagreements with their mothers about completing household chores and issues surrounding dating (e.g., whether or not they can go on dates or have a boyfriend) and their appearance (e.g., what clothes they wear, whether they can wear make-up), with effect sizes ranging from $d = .49$ to $d = .62$. Smaller, but still significant, differences emerged in disagreements about being respectful to parents and disobeying household rules, d's $= .30$ and .31, respectively, with more frequent conflicts between Juntos adolescents and their mothers than between

Table 4.3. Adolescent Reports of Conflicts by Topic for Supporting MAMI and Juntos Projects

Topics of Conflict	MAMI Project ($n = 179$) M	SD	Juntos Project ($n = 78$) M	SD	F
Chores	2.40	1.35	3.28	1.48	21.76***
Appearance	1.73	1.20	2.38	1.46	14.00***
Homework and schoolwork	2.15	1.35	2.36	1.29	
Friends	2.30	1.50	2.23	1.31	
Bedtime and curfew	2.31	1.43	2.51	1.31	
Respect for parents	2.18	1.23	2.58	1.42	5.13*
Getting along with siblings	2.82	1.66	3.05	1.54	
Family time	1.89	1.38	2.06	1.39	
Romantic relationships	1.72	1.19	2.12	1.34	5.55*
Disobeying rules	2.03	1.07	2.73	1.38	19.54***

Note: F-test values were only included for significant group differences.
*$p < .05$. **$p < .01$. ***$p < .001$.

Supporting MAMI adolescents and their mothers. Consistent with the overall pattern that mothers in the Supporting MAMI and Juntos projects did not differ in their reports of the frequency of conflicts with daughters, mothers also did not differ in the frequency of disagreements about specific conflict topics. We also asked adolescents and mothers in the Supporting MAMI project how frequently they had disagreements related to adolescents' pregnancy. Adolescents and their mothers reported pregnancy-related disagreements occurring slightly below the midpoint of the scale ($M = 2.28$; $SD = 1.51$ for adolescents' reports and $M = 2.37$; $SD = 1.53$ for mothers' reports).

Turning to cultural backgrounds and orientations, mothers in both the Supporting MAMI and Juntos projects were more likely to be born in Mexico than in the U.S. In contrast, adolescents in the Juntos Project were significantly more likely to be born in Mexico than were adolescents in the Supporting MAMI project. Despite differences in girls' nativity, adolescents in both groups reported similar levels of Mexican and Anglo cultural orientations. Overall, girls in these two samples reported strong involvement in Mexican culture (i.e., slightly below 4.0 on a 5-point scale) and relatively high levels of involvement in Anglo culture (i.e., above 3.50 on a 5-point scale). Mothers reported similarly high levels of Mexican orientations as their daughters (i.e., averaging above 4.0/5.0), but lower Anglo orientations than their daughters (around the midpoint of the scale). In both groups, mothers and daughters differed significantly in their Anglo orientations, but not in their Mexican orientations.

Adolescents in both groups were similar in their levels of depressive symptoms, scoring around the midpoint of the scale. Mothers, on the other hand, significantly differed in their reports of depressive symptoms, with mothers in the MAMI project reporting more depressive symptoms than mothers in the Juntos project, $d = .68$. In terms of risky behavior, girls in the MAMI project reported higher levels of engagement in risky behavior than did girls in the Juntos project, $d = .28$.

Goal 1: Mother–Daughter Conflict and Adjustment. We conducted regression analyses to examine the associations between mother–daughter conflict and risky behaviors and to test the moderating role of family context. The first step included control variables (i.e., income, family structure, and adolescent nativity) to account for sample differences in these background characteristics, the second step included main effects (i.e., mother–adolescent conflict, family context), and the third step included the interaction between mother–adolescent conflict and family context. Following Aiken and West (1991), variables were centered prior to creating the interaction term.

For adolescents' depressive symptoms, no significant predictors emerged in the first step, but adolescents' reports of mother–adolescent conflict were positively associated with girls' depressive symptoms, $\beta = .18$, $p < .01$, with the model accounting for 5% of the variance, $F(5,231) =$

2.21, $p < .05$. Family context did not moderate the links between conflict and depressive symptoms. For mothers' reports of depressive symptoms, family income was a significant predictor in the first step, accounting for 16% of the variance. In particular, mothers with more economic resources reported lower levels of depressive symptoms, $\beta = -.18$, $p < .05$. In the second step, mothers' reports of mother–adolescent conflict and family context were significant predictors, with the model accounting for 21% of the variance, $F(5, 232) = 12.25$, $p < .00$. As noted earlier, mothers in the MAMI project reported more depressive symptoms than did mothers in the Juntos project, $\beta = -.21$, $p < .01$. In addition, mothers who reported more conflict with daughters also reported more depressive symptoms, $\beta = .11$, $p < .01$. Family context did not emerge as a significant moderator.

The model predicting adolescents' risky behaviors also was significant. In the first step, adolescent nativity was a significant predictor, accounting for 5% of the variance, $F(3, 234) = 4.36$, $p < .01$. Consistent with prior work (Gonzales, Knight, Morgan-Lopez, Saenz, & Sirolli, 2002), U.S.-born girls reported higher involvement in risky behavior than Mexico-born girls, $\beta = -.18$, $p < .01$. In the second step, adolescents' reports of mother–daughter conflict and family context were significant predictors, with the model accounting for 24% of the variance, $F(3, 232) = 27.70$, $p < .01$. Specifically, girls in the MAMI project described higher levels of risky behaviors than did girls in the Juntos project, $\beta = -.20$, $p < .01$, and mother–daughter conflict was positively associated with risky behaviors, $\beta = .20$, $p < .01$. Family context did not moderate the conflict–risky behavior association.

Goal 2: Conflict-Adjustment Links and Discrepancies in Cultural Orientations. To test whether adolescent–mother differences in cultural orientations moderated conflict-adjustment linkages and whether differences emerged as a function of family context, we added 2-way interactions (e.g., Conflict × Family Context, Mexican Orientation Discrepancy × Family Context, Conflict × Mexican Orientation Discrepancy) and the 3-way interaction (e.g., Conflict × Mexican Orientation Discrepancy × Family Context) to the prior regression models. We tested for the role of discrepancies in Mexican and Anglo orientations separately.

For the model including adolescent–mother differences in Mexican orientations to predict adolescent risky behaviors, the interaction between mother–adolescent conflict as reported by adolescents and adolescent–mother differences in Mexican orientations was significant and accounted for significant increase in the variance explained, F change $(3,221) = 2.58$, $p < .05$, $\Delta R^2 = .03$. The model accounted for 27% of the variance in risky behaviors, $F(9, 221) = 8.83$, $p < .00$. To follow-up, we examined the association between conflict and adjustment when the difference score was one standard deviation above the mean (i.e., adolescents scored higher on Mexican orientations than mothers, $n = 21$), at the mean (i.e., adolescents and mothers reported similar Mexican orientations, $n = 172$), and one

Figure 4.1. Association between conflict and risky behaviors as moderated by adolescent–mother differences in Mexican orientations

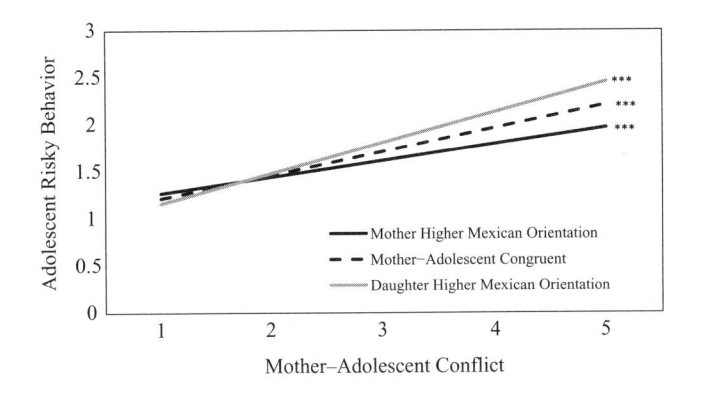

[Figure: Line graph with x-axis "Mother–Adolescent Conflict" (1 to 5) and y-axis "Adolescent Risky Behavior" (0 to 3). Three lines: Mother Higher Mexican Orientation (***), Mother–Adolescent Congruent (***), Daughter Higher Mexican Orientation (***).]

Note: $*p < .05.$ $**p < .01.$ $***p < .001.$

standard deviation below the mean (i.e., mothers reported higher Mexican orientations than adolescents, $n = 64$). The overall samples' average of Mexican orientation incongruence was $M = -0.18$ ($SD = 0.65$). The positive association between mother–adolescent conflict and risky behavior was significant for all three groups, but strongest when adolescents reported higher levels of Mexican orientations than their mothers (see Figure 4.1). The pattern of associations did not differ as a function of family context. No new predictors emerged in the models predicting adolescents' or mothers' depressive symptoms.

Turning to the model including mother–daughter differences in *Anglo orientations*, the 3-way interaction (i.e., Conflict × Family Context × Adolescent–Mother Anglo orientation difference score) was significant for both adolescents' depressive symptoms and risky behaviors. Follow-up analyses on the 3-way interaction revealed that adolescent–mother differences in Anglo orientations moderated the associations between conflict and adjustment for adolescents in the Juntos project, but not for adolescents in the Supporting MAMI project. For Juntos project adolescents, we examined the association between conflict and adjustment using one standard deviation above and below the mean as cutoffs. The average difference between adolescents and mothers in their Anglo orientations was .98 ($SD = .95$), and the result was the following three groups: (1) mother–adolescent congruence in Anglo orientations (i.e., a difference score of .03 and lower, $n = 11$); (2) moderate discrepancy (i.e., difference score was between 1 standard deviation below and above the mean, above .03 and below 1.93, reflecting adolescents' higher Anglo orientations as compared

Figure 4.2. Association between conflict and depressive symptoms for the Juntos sample as moderated by adolescent–mother differences in Anglo orientations

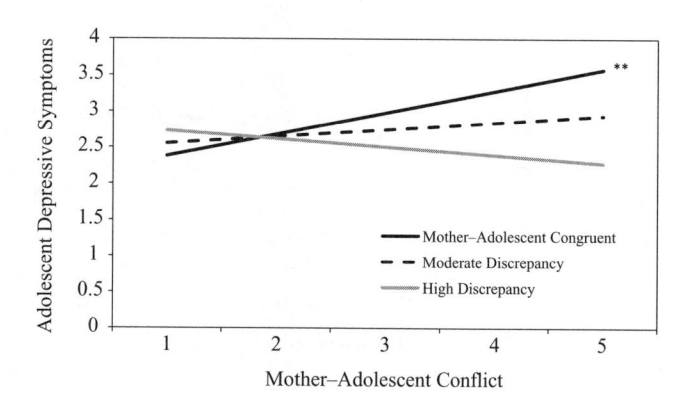

Note: Discrepancies reflected daughters reporting higher Anglo orientations than mothers.
$*p < .05.$ $**p < .01.$ $***p < .001.$

Figure 4.3. Association between conflict and risky behaviors for the Juntos sample as moderated by adolescent–mother differences in Anglo orientations. Discrepancies reflected daughters reporting higher Anglo orientations than mothers.

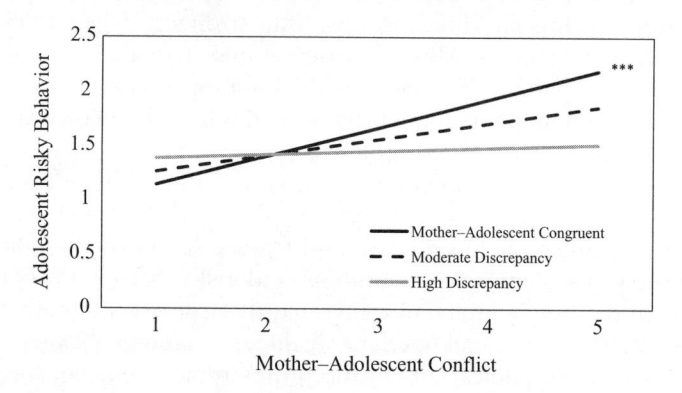

Note: $*p < .05.$ $**p < .01.$ $***p < .001.$

to mothers', $n = 56$); and (3) high discrepancy (i.e., difference score was 1 standard deviation above the mean, i.e., above 1.93, reflecting adolescents as much more Anglo oriented than their mothers, $n = 11$). The conflict-adjustment association was significant only for the congruent group for both adolescents' depressive symptoms (Figure 4.2) and risky behaviors (Figure 4.3). Turning to mothers' depressive symptoms, we found significant main effects for family context and mother–adolescent conflict (both described earlier), and in addition, a main effect for the Anglo orientation difference score (i.e., adolescents' Anglo orientations minus mothers' Anglo orientations) was significant, accounting for 22% of the variance, $F(6, 224) = 10.01$, $p < .00$. Specifically, when adolescents described being more Anglo-oriented than mothers (i.e., higher positive difference scores), mothers reported higher levels of depressive symptoms, $\beta = .07$, $p < .05$.

Discussion

Conflict between parents and adolescents over everyday family life, such as completing homework, helping out around the house, and getting along with sisters and brothers, is viewed as normative in adolescence among families from a range of cultural backgrounds (e.g., Fuligni, 1998; Laursen & Collins, 2004; Smetana & Gaines, 1999). In Latino families, family conflict, including intergenerational conflicts, has been associated with increased youth adjustment problems, including higher levels of depression, anxiety, and misconduct (Lau et al., 2005; Pasch et al., 2006; Updegraff et al., 2009). We contributed to the literature on conflict-adjustment linkages in Latino families of Mexican origin by examining how the family and sociocultural contexts may exacerbate or reduce associations between parent–adolescent conflict and youth and parent adjustment problems. Our findings illustrate how the family context, as defined by the transition to adolescent motherhood, and the sociocultural context, as measured by intergenerational discrepancies in cultural orientations, were associated with variations in conflict-adjustment linkages.

Mother–Daughter Conflict in Mexican-Origin Families. Little attention has been paid to normative developmental and family processes among ethnic minority youth (McLoyd, 1998), and we know even less about normative development among ethnic minority adolescents who are facing the transition to motherhood in combination with the transition through adolescence (Contreras, 2004). With regard to the occurrence of conflicts over everyday topics, such as chores, Mexican-origin girls in both samples reported low to moderate levels of disagreements with their mothers. Girls in the Juntos project, who were not preparing for the transition to motherhood, reported more daily conflict with their mothers than girls in the Supporting MAMI project. In particular, conflicts about helping around the house, dating, and appearance were less salient for girls in the Supporting MAMI project. Girls who are transitioning to adolescent motherhood may be less focused on normative topics of conflict (chores, appearance) given their focus on preparing for motherhood and pregnancy-related issues as sources of unique conflict for these girls and their mothers. It is notable that mothers in the two samples did not perceive differences in the frequency of conflict overall or about specific topics.

These within-family (i.e., mother–daughter) differences point to the importance of considering the perceptions of different family members (e.g., in levels of conflict or how conflicts are resolved—see Cookston et al., current volume) and the implications of such differences for family dynamics.

For pregnant adolescents, we also found that disagreements occurred with their mothers about issues related to their pregnancy (e.g., how well they were taking care of themselves), although not with high frequency. It may be important to extend ideas about normative conflicts in families negotiating the transition to adolescent motherhood to include conflicts around issues that are specific to pregnancy, parenthood, and the role of the baby's biological father, as these topics may be more salient for mother–daughter dyads facing the transition to adolescent motherhood. Given that the majority of young Latina mothers turn to their own mothers for support (Contreras et al., 2002), it will be important to understand the nature of conflicts that arise as a result of negotiating co-parenting roles and how such conflicts contribute to adolescents' and their mothers' well-being.

Mexican-Origin Adolescents' and Mothers' Well-Being. Our findings regarding differences across the samples in depressive symptoms also underscore the significance of within-family (i.e., mother–daughter) differences. Adolescents reported similar levels of depressive symptoms, regardless of the family context, but mothers in the Supporting MAMI project reported more depressive symptoms than did mothers in the Juntos project. These differences were accounted for, in part, by socioeconomic resources, as mothers in the Supporting MAMI project described lower household incomes than mothers in the Juntos project, and household income was a significant predictor of mothers' depressive symptoms. Family context, however, was a significant predictor of mothers' depressive symptoms after accounting for background differences between the two samples. It is important to consider that, for these mothers, their daughters' early transition to parenthood may be a source of stress and have implications for their own well-being. Given that mothers are important providers of emotional and instrumental support as their daughters become mothers in middle to late adolescence (Contreras et al., 2002), understanding the factors that contribute to these mothers' ability to successfully navigate this family transition deserves further consideration.

In addition, adolescents in the Supporting MAMI project reported engaging in risky behaviors more often than adolescents in the Juntos project, although the effect size was small. These differences may reflect pregnant adolescents' co-involvement in different types of risk-taking behaviors, including those we assessed in our general measure of risky behaviors (e.g., getting in trouble at school or with authority figures, drinking alcohol or smoking), along with early engagement in sexual behaviors that resulted in pregnancy. It is also possible that adolescent girls making the early transition to motherhood affiliate with peers who are engaging in a variety of deviant behaviors, contributing to their own engagement in risky behaviors.

Within-Family Similarities and Differences in Cultural Orientations. Adolescent girls and their mothers (in both samples) described high levels of involvement in Mexican culture, indicating fluency and usage of Spanish, celebration of Mexican cultural traditions, and associations with same-ethnic peers. Further, adolescents and their mothers reported *similar* levels of cultural involvement reflecting a group of families with strong intergenerational ties to Mexican culture. This may result partly from the sample's geographic location. That is, these families lived in a well-established Mexican American community in a southwestern state that borders Mexico. The strong representation of Mexican heritage individuals in this region and the close proximity to Mexico may promote strong ties to the ethnic culture that may be less likely in other geographic locations in the United States.

It is notable that adolescents, but not mothers, also described moderate levels of involvement in U.S. culture. A likely result of attending school in the U.S., girls in this sample also indicated fluency in English and involvement with mainstream culture and peers. Girls differed significantly from their mothers in their Anglo orientations, suggesting that girls in both samples maintained strong ties to Mexican culture but also were involved in U.S. culture. Their mothers, in contrast, maintained strong ethnic ties but were less likely to be involved in U.S. culture. These findings are consistent with the perspective that cultural adaptation is multidimensional (Berry, 2003), as considering either Mexican or Anglo orientations in isolation would have led us to different conclusions about the intergenerational discrepancies between mothers and daughters.

The Role of the Family and Sociocultural Context. We explored the possibility that the connections between mother–adolescent conflict and mothers' and daughters' adjustment may be stronger as a function of family context, as defined by families experiencing the transition to adolescent motherhood as compared with same-aged adolescents and their mothers who were not preparing for the transition to adolescent motherhood. We did not find, however, that the association differed significantly for these two groups of adolescent–mother dyads. Frequency of conflict was associated with adolescents' and mothers' depressive symptoms, accounting for a small percentage of the variance, and also with adolescents' risky behaviors, accounting for more moderate levels of variance. Findings are consistent with other work highlighting the concurrent associations between parent–adolescent conflict and youth well-being (Lau et al., 2005; Pasch et al., 2006; Updegraff et al., 2009). Less is known about the role of conflict in *parent* well-being in Mexican American families, however. Insights about how parent–child relationship processes affect *both* adolescent *and* parent well-being in Mexican American families is a topic that warrants further consideration.

With respect to mother–daughter discrepancies on indices of cultural orientation, research on the implications of intergenerational discrepancies in cultural adaptation processes has resulted in inconsistent support for the associations between parent–child differences in cultural characteristics and problems in the parent–youth relationship, and in turn, youth adjustment (Birman, 2006). Inconsistent findings may be attributed to different methodological approaches to assessing intergenerational differences, and particularly, to the limited number of studies that measure *actual* discrepancies in cultural characteristics using data from multiple family members (Birman, 2006). A strength of our approach was that we used reports of cultural orientations from adolescents *and* their mothers to capture within-family differences in Mexican and Anglo cultural orientations. Cultural discrepancies may be particularly important in adolescence, a time when adolescents become more active agents in their cultural socialization (as compared to earlier developmental periods) and when adolescents have more autonomy to choose how and with whom they spend their time (Umaña-Taylor & Fine, 2004).

Our findings revealed different patterns for Mexican versus Anglo orientation discrepancies, again highlighting the multidimensional nature of cultural adaptation in families (Berry, 2003). Beginning with Mexican orientations, the positive association between mother–daughter conflict and adolescents' risky behavior was strongest in families where adolescent girls were more Mexican-oriented than their mothers. The association was significant, but weaker, in families where mothers and adolescents described similar levels of Mexican orientations, and significant but weakest, in families where mothers were more Mexican-oriented than adolescents. One interpretation is that families characterized by adolescents who have stronger Mexican orientations than their mothers are nonnormative (i.e., less common) in this cultural context (Updegraff et al., 2006), and thus, have more limited social support for handling the stressors in their relationships, strengthening the association between mother–daughter conflict and adolescent adjustment problems. Predictions about normative patterns of cultural adaptation lead to the expectation that parents will retain stronger ties to Mexican culture than their offspring (Portes & Rumbaut, 2001; Szapocznik & Kurtines, 1980, 1993), suggesting that families characterized by more Mexican-oriented mothers than daughters may be normative. In these families' everyday lives, incongruence in Mexican orientations favoring adolescents over their mothers may be a *person– environment mismatch* (Eccles et al., 1993; Lerner & Lerner, 1983), placing these girls at increased risk for adjustment difficulties.

Discrepancies in mothers' and adolescents' Anglo orientations also moderated the links between mother–daughter conflict and daughters' risky behaviors and depressive symptoms, but only for mother–daughter dyads who were *not* preparing for the transition to adolescent motherhood. These findings also can be interpreted to reflect the potential negative implications of person–environment mismatch (Eccles et al., 1993). Specifically, when mothers and daughters described similar levels of Anglo orientations, higher levels of mother–daughter conflict were associated with girls' more frequent engagement in risky behavior and higher levels of depressive symptoms. In contrast, when daughters were more Anglo-oriented than their mothers, the association between mother–daughter conflict and adjustment was not significant. With respect to intergenerational discrepancies in Anglo orientations, it would be expected that adolescents would have stronger orientations than their mothers, as a result of their exposure to the U.S. education system and the earlier developmental timing of their immigration to the United States (as compared to their parents). Similarities in mothers' and daughters' Anglo orientations, however, may be nonnormative within this sociocultural context, and thus, elevate the risks associated with mother–daughter conflict for adolescent girls. Our findings suggest that mother–daughter cultural discrepancies must be understood within the broader context of families' lives. When discrepancies are consistent with cultural norms of the context (e.g., youth being more acculturated than parents), parents and youth may have more resources and support systems to negotiate their differences, and their discrepancies may not be associated with youth adjustment problems. It is important to note that discrepancies in Anglo orientations did not moderate conflict-adjustment linkages for mothers and daughters preparing for the transition to adolescent motherhood. In these families, discrepancies in Anglo orientations may be less salient than the preparation for changes in the family system surrounding the transition to early parenthood.

A different pattern emerged for mothers. Higher discrepancies in Anglo orientations were associated with mothers' depressive symptoms, such that when daughters reported higher Anglo orientations relative to their mothers, mothers reported higher levels of depressive symptoms. These findings are consistent with the idea that when youth acculturate at a faster rate than their parents, families are at risk for adjustment difficulties (Portes & Rumbaut, 2001; Szapocznik & Kurtines, 1980, 1993). It is notable, though, that the preponderance of this work focuses on the implications for *youth* adjustment and much less is known about the consequences for *parent* well-being. Importantly, these findings alert us to the need to consider how cultural discrepancies are linked to the health and well-being of *both* parents *and* youth in immigrant families.

Conclusion

The findings presented in the current chapter extend research on conflict-adjustment linkages in Mexican-origin families in several important ways. First, they highlight the complex role of the characteristics of the family and sociocultural context in shaping the associations between mother–daughter conflict and adolescents' and mothers' concurrent adjustment. It will be important to examine these associations longitudinally to capture developmental, family, and cultural adaptation processes over time and to link these processes to trajectories of well-being (e.g., increases in depressive symptoms or risk-taking behaviors). Our study focused on mothers with daughters in middle to late adolescence, but it will be important to explore how these associations may differ across the course of adolescence and into young adulthood. Second, our focus on adolescents' and mothers' Mexican and Anglo cultural orientations provided a more complete picture of the role of cultural discrepancies in conflict-adjustment linkages than a focus on either dimension in isolation. Cultural values, such as familism values, also may be sources of within-family variation and deserve consideration in future work. Finally, findings revealed differential links from parent–adolescent and cultural discrepancy processes to adolescents' versus mothers' well-being, underscoring the need to consider how these processes may be differentially associated with well-being for different family members. It will be important to replicate and extend this work to increase our understanding of within-family differences in the implications of family dynamics and cultural adaptation for parent and youth well-being.

References

Aiken, L. S., & West, S. G. (1991). *Multiple regression: Testing and interpreting interactions*. Newbury Park, CA: Sage.

Berry, J. W. (2003). Conceptual approaches to acculturation. In K. M. Chun, P. B. Organista, & G. Marín (Eds.), *Acculturation: Advances in theory, measurement, and applied research* (pp. 17–38). Washington, DC: American Psychological Association.

Birman, D. (2006). Measurement of the "acculturation gap" in immigrant families and implications for parent-child relationships. In M. Bornstein & L. Cotes (Eds.), *Acculturation and parent-child relationships: Measurement and development* (pp. 113–134). Hillsdale, NJ: Erlbaum.

Bronfenbrenner, U., & Crouter, A. C. (1983). The evolution of environment modes in development research. In P. H. Mussen (Ed.), *Handbook of child psychology* (Vol. 1, pp. 358–414). New York, NY: Wiley.

Cauce, A. M., & Domenech-Rodríguez, M. (2002). Latino families: Myths and realities. In J. M. Contreras, K. A. Kerns, & A. M. Neal-Barnett (Eds.), *Latino children and families in the United States: Current research and future directions* (pp. 3–26). Westport, CT: Praeger.

Cohen, J. (1988). *Statistical power analysis for the behavioral sciences*. Hillsdale, NJ: Erlbaum.

Contreras, J. M. (2004). Parenting behaviors among mainland Puerto Rican adolescent mothers: The role of grandmother and partner involvement. *Journal of Research on Adolescence, 14*, 341–368. doi: 10.1111/j.1532-7795.2004.00078.x

Contreras, J. M., Narang, D., Ikhlas, M., & Teichman, J. (2002). A conceptual model of the determinants of parenting among Latina adolescent mothers. In J. M. Contreras, K. A. Kerns, & A. M. Neal-Barnett (Eds.), *Latino children and families in the United States: Current research and future directions* (pp. 155–177). Westport, CT: Praeger.

Cookston, J. T., Olide, A. F., Adams, M., Fabricius, W. V., Parke, R. D. (2012). Guided cognitive reframing of adolescent–father conflict: Who Mexican American and European American adolescents seek and why. In L. P. Juang & A. J. Umaña-Taylor (Eds.), *Family conflict among Chinese- and Mexican-origin adolescents and their parents in the U.S. New Directions for Child and Adolescent Development, 135,* 83–103.
Crouter, A. C., Manke, B. A., & McHale, S. M. (1995). The family context of gender intensification in early adolescence. *Child Development, 66,* 317–329. doi: 10.2307/1131580
Cuéllar, I., Arnold, B., & Maldonado, R. (1995). Acculturation Rating Scale for Mexican Americans-II: A revision of the original ARSMA scale. *Hispanic Journal of Behavioral Sciences, 17,* 275–304. doi:10.1177/07399863950173001
Eccles, J. S., & Barber, B. (1990). *Risky behavior measure.* Ann Arbor, MI: University of Michigan.
Eccles, J. S., Midgley, C., Wigfield, A., Buchanan, C. M., Reuman, D., Flanagan, C., & Iver, D. M. (1993). Development during adolescence: The impact of stage-environment fit on young adolescents' experiences in schools and in families. *American Psychologist, 48,* 90–101. doi: 10.1037/10254-034
Erikson, E. H. (1968). *Identity: Youth and crisis.* New York, NY: Norton.
Fuligni, A. (1998). Authority, autonomy, and parent-adolescent conflict and cohesion: A study of adolescents from Mexican, Chinese, Filipino, and European backgrounds. *Developmental Psychology, 34,* 782–792. doi: 10.1037/0012-1649.34.4.782
García Coll, C. G., Crnic, K., Lamberty, G., Waskik, B. H., Jenkins, R., Garcia, H. V., & McAdoo, H.P. (1996). An integrative model for the study of developmental competencies in minority children. *Child Development, 67,* 1891–1914. doi: 10.2307/1131600
Gonzales, N. A., German, M., Kim, S. Y., George, P., Fabrett, F. C., Milsap, R., & Dunka, L. E. (2008). Mexican American adolescents' cultural orientation, externalizing behavior and academic engagement: The role of traditional cultural values. *American Journal of Community Psychology, 41,* 151–164. doi: 10.1007/s10464-007-9152-x
Gonzales, N. A., Knight, G. P., Morgan-Lopez, A. A., Saenz, D., & Sirolli, A. (2002). Acculturation and the mental health of Latino youths: An integration and critique of the literature. In J. M. Contreras, K. A. Kerns, & A. M. Neal-Barnett (Eds.), *Latino children and families in the United States: Current research and future directions* (pp. 45–74). Westport, CT: Praeger.
Harris, V. S. (1992). But dad said I could: Within-family differences in parental control in early adolescence. *Dissertation Abstracts International, 52,* 4104.
Hill, J. P., & Lynch, M. E. (1983). The intensification of gender-related role expectations during early adolescence. In J. Brooks-Gunn & A. Petersen (Eds.), *Girls at puberty: Biological and psychosocial perspectives* (pp. 201–228). New York, NY: Plenum Press.
Knight, G. P., Roosa, M. W., & Umaña-Taylor, A. J. (2009). *Studying ethnic minority and economically disadvantaged populations: Methodological challenges and best practices.* Washington, DC: APA Books.
Lau, A. S., McCabe, K. M., Yeh, M., Garland, A. F., Wood, P. A., & Hough, R. L. (2005). The acculturation gap-distress hypothesis among high-risk Mexican American families. *Journal of Family Psychology, 19,* 367–375. doi: 10.1037/0893-3200.19.3.367
Laursen, B. (2005). Conflict between mothers and adolescents in single-mother, blended, and two-biological parent families. *Parenting: Science and Practice, 5*(4), 247–270. doi: 10.1207/s15327922par0504_3
Laursen, B., & Collins, W. A. (2004). Parent-child communication during adolescence. In B. Laursen & W. A. Collins (Eds.), *Handbook of family communication* (pp. 333–348). Mahwah, NJ: Erlbaum.
Lerner, J. V., & Lerner, R. M. (1983). Temperament and adaptation across life: Theoretical and empirical issues. In P. B. Baltes & O. G. Brim (Eds.), *Lifespan development and behavior* (pp. 197–231) New York, NY: Academic Press.

Marcia, J. (1994). The empirical study of ego identity. In H. A. Bosma, T.L.G. Graafsman, H. D. Grotevant, & D. J. De Levita (Eds.), *Identity and development* (pp. 281–321). Newbury Park, CA: Sage.

Marín, G., & Marín, B. V. (1991). *Research with Hispanic populations.* Newbury Park, CA: Sage Publications.

Markus, H. J., & Wurf, E. (1987). The dynamic self-concept: A social psychological perspective. *Annual Review of Psychology, 38,* 299–331. doi: 10.1146/annurev.ps.38.020187.001503

McLoyd, V. C. (1998). Changing demographics in the American population: Implications for research on minority children and adolescents. In V. C. McLoyd & L. Steinberg (Eds.), *Studying minority adolescents: Conceptual, methodological, and theoretical issues* (pp. 3–28). Mahwah, NJ: Erlbaum.

National Vital Statistics Report. (2005). Births: Final data for 2003. Atlanta, GA: Centers for Disease Control and Prevention, National Center for Health Statistics. Retrieved from http://www.cdc.gov/nchs/data/nvsr/nvsr54/nvsr54_02.pdf.

Pasch, L. A., Deardorff, J., Tschann, J. M., Flores, E., Penilla, C., & Pantoja, P. (2006). Acculturation, parent-adolescent conflict, and adolescent adjustment in Mexican American families. *Family Process, 45,* 75–86. doi: 10.1111/j.1545-5300.2006.00081.x

Portes, A., & Rumbaut, R. G. 2001. *The story of the immigrant second generation: Legacies.* Los Angeles, CA: University of California Press.

Radloff, L. (1977). The CES-D Scale: A self-report depression scale for research in the general population. *Applied Psychological Measurement, 1*(3), 385–401. doi: 10.1177/014662167700100306

Scaramella, L. V., & Conger. R. D. (2004). Continuity versus discontinuity in parent and adolescent negative affect. In R. D. Conger, F. O. Lorenz, & K.A.S. Wickrama (Eds.), *Continuity and change in family relations: Theory, methods, and empirical findings* (pp. 241–265). Mahwah, NJ: Erlbaum.

Smetana, J. G. (1988). Adolescents' and parents' conceptions of parental authority. *Child Development, 59,* 321–335. doi: 10.2307/1130313

Smetana, J., & Gaines, C. (1999). Adolescent-parent conflict in middle-class African American families. *Child Development, 70,* 1447–1463. doi: 10.1111/1467-8624.00105

Szapocznik, J., & Kurtines, W. (1980). Acculturation, biculturalism, and adjustment. In A. Padilla (Ed.), *Recent advances in acculturation research* (pp. 139–159). New York, NY: Westview Press.

Szapocznik, J., & Kurtines, W. M. (1993). Family psychology and cultural diversity: Opportunities of theory, research, and application. *American Psychologist, 48,* 400–407.

Umaña-Taylor, A. J., & Fine, M. A. (2004). Examining a model of ethnic identity development among Mexican-origin adolescents living in the U.S. *Hispanic Journal of Behavioral Sciences, 26,* 36–59. doi:10.1177/0739986303262143

Umaña-Taylor, A. J., & Alfaro, E. C. (2009). Acculturative stress and adaptation. In F. A. Villaruel, G. Carlo, J. M. Grau, M. Azmitia, N. Cabrera, & T. J. Chahin (Eds.), *Handbook of Latino psychology* (pp. 135–152). Thousand Oaks, CA: Sage.

Updegraff, K. A., Delgado, M. Y., & Wheeler, L. A. (2009). Exploring mothers' and fathers' relationships with sons versus daughters: Links to adolescent adjustment in Mexican immigrant families. *Sex Roles, 60,* 559–574. doi: 10.1007/s11199-008-9527-y

Updegraff, K. A., McHale, S. M., Crouter, A. C., & Kupanoff, K. (2001). Parents' involvement in adolescents' peer relationships: A comparison of mothers' and fathers' roles. *Journal of Marriage and Family, 63,* 655–668. doi: 10.1111/j.1741-3737.2001.00655.x

Updegraff, K. A., McHale, S. M., Whiteman, S. D., Thayer, S. M., & Crouter, A. C. (2006). The nature and correlates of Mexican American adolescents' time with parents and peers. *Child Development, 77,* 1470–1486. doi: 10.1111/j.1467-8624.2006.00948.x

Updegraff, K. A., McHale, S. M., Whiteman, S. D., Thayer, S. M., & Delgado, M. Y. (2005). Adolescent sibling relationships in Mexican American families: Exploring the role of familism. *Journal of Family Psychology, 19,* 512–522. doi: 10.1037/0893-3200.19.4.512

Whitman, T. L., Borkowski, J. G., Keogh, D., & Weed, K. (2001). *Interwoven lives: Adolescent mothers and their children.* Mahwah, NJ: Erlbaum.

KIMBERLY A. UPDEGRAFF is a professor in the School of Social and Family Dynamics at Arizona State University, Tempe. E-mail: Kimberly.updegraff @asu.edu

ADRIANA J. UMAÑA-TAYLOR is an associate professor in the School of Social and Family Dynamics at Arizona State University, Tempe. E-mail: Adriana. Umana-Taylor@asu.edu

NORMA J. PEREZ-BRENA is a graduate student in the School of Social and Family Dynamics at Arizona State University, Tempe. E-mail: Nperezbr@asu.edu

JACQUELINE PFLIEGER is a senior associate at ICF International, Survey and Evaluation Research Center, Fairfax, VA. E-mail: jpflieger@icfi.com

Cookston, J. T., Olide, A. F., Adams, M. A., Fabricius, W. V., Parke, R. D. (2012). Guided cognitive reframing of adolescent–father conflict: Who Mexican American and European American adolescents seek and why. In L. P. Juang & A. J. Umaña-Taylor (Eds.), *Family conflict among Chinese- and Mexican-origin adolescents and their parents in the U.S. New Directions for Child and Adolescent Development, 135*, 83–103.

5

Guided Cognitive Reframing of Adolescent–Father Conflict: Who Mexican American and European American Adolescents Seek and Why

Jeffrey T. Cookston, Andres F. Olide, Michele A. Adams, William V. Fabricius, Ross D. Parke

Abstract

Adolescents may seek to understand family conflict by seeking out confidants. However, little is known about whom adolescents seek, whether and how such support helps youth, and the factors that predict which sources are sought. This chapter offers a conceptual model of guided cognitive reframing that emphasizes the behavioral, cognitive, and affective implications of confidant support as well as individual, family, and cultural factors linked to support seeking. The authors present empirical data from 392 families of seventh graders of Mexican and European ancestry to predict whether adolescents seek mothers, coresident fathers, and other sources and provide directions for subsequent research. © 2012 Wiley Periodicals, Inc.

We wish to acknowledge the families who participated in this study, the National Institute of Mental Health Grant 5R01MH064829, and our many colleagues on the project.

Conflict between adolescents and their parents is an important predictor of adolescent adjustment (Gonzales, Deardorff, Formoso, Barr, & Barrera, 2006), and seeking social support to cope with conflict is healthy for adolescents (Nomaguchi, 2008). However, little is known about the psychological experience that social support plays in the lives of adolescents and what explains whether adolescents seek different sources of support. The choice to seek out others for support, the information sources provide, and the emotional consequences of those interactions are important to adolescents as they attempt to understand conflict interactions in their lives. We term this process guided cognitive reframing. In this chapter, we first offer a behavioral-cognitive-affective conceptual model for guided cognitive reframing that links seeking out a source of support, engaging in cognitive reframing of the conflict, and the affective experiences that result from reframing. Next, we review the literature on the confidants that adolescents seek (and the relative advantage of seeking each source). Finally, because the majority of the extant research has focused on adolescents in European American families, we examine cultural context, family, and individual factors that explain who is sought out to discuss family conflict among a diverse sample of Mexican American and European American seventh graders.

An Overview of Guided Cognitive Reframing: A Model for Understanding Coping and Support of Parent–Adolescent Conflict

Whereas middle childhood tends to be comparatively conflict-free, early adolescence is a time of increasing parent–child conflict (Granic, Hollenstein, Dishion & Patterson, 2003). However, despite evidence for the apparent links between high levels of parent–adolescent conflict and adolescent adjustment (Barber & Delfabbro, 2000; Chung, Flook, & Fuligni, 2009; Juang, Syed, Cookston, Wang, & Kim, current volume; Updegraff et al., current volume), less is known about how adolescents make sense of the conflict they have with their parents. Although responses to stress are diverse, the coping literature suggests two common ways of managing reactions to a stressful event (Connor-Smith, Compas, Wadsworth, Thomsen, & Saltzman, 2000). Active-approach coping involves engaging a stressor event (e.g., problem solving) and has been linked to more desirable adjustment (DeCarlo Santiago & Wadsworth, 2009; Rogers & Holmbeck, 1997). A second approach, namely disengaging from a stressor event (e.g., denying, avoiding), has been linked to more risky outcomes (Ohannessian, Bradley, Waninger, Ruddy, Hepp, & Hesselbrock, 2010; Wadsworth, Raviv, Compas, & Connor-Smith, 2005).

Although the coping literature delineates styles of coping, the cognitive-motivational-relational theory of Lazarus (1991) provides a useful theoretical framework for understanding the effects of variations in seeking out different sources to discuss family conflict. According to this theory, an emotion-evoking situation results in a cognitive appraisal that is evaluated for self-relevance. If an event is seen as self-relevant, other appraisals determine whether the situation threatens one's status and whether one is to blame for the event which, in turn, leads to the planning of a behavioral response. Lazarus's model of appraisals in relationships offers a perspective on how guided cognitive reframing might be adaptive for adolescents. Specifically, according to Lazarus (1991) and the coping literature, an active coping strategy like seeking out a source for support should result in changed cognitions about the conflict partner (e.g., the reason for the conflict, whether the conflict partner is to blame for the event). Additionally, these reinterpreted cognitive explanations should explain how the adolescent feels after seeking a reframing agent (e.g., better self-evaluations and evaluations of the conflict partner).

According to our conceptualization of guided cognitive reframing (Figure 5.1), we anticipate that cognitions associated with more frequent reframing events will explain changes in affective evaluations and will be uniquely linked to child adjustment. In our conceptualization, we anticipate that talking with others about conflict will be related to changes in cognitive interpretations of the conflict because adolescents will gain a better understanding of (1) the reason for the conflict, and (2) whether the adolescent is responsible for the conflict. These cognitions, in turn, should be related to affective evaluations of the self and the conflict partner. In this light, we view guided cognitive reframing as an active coping

Figure 5.1. Conceptual model of guided cognitive reframing

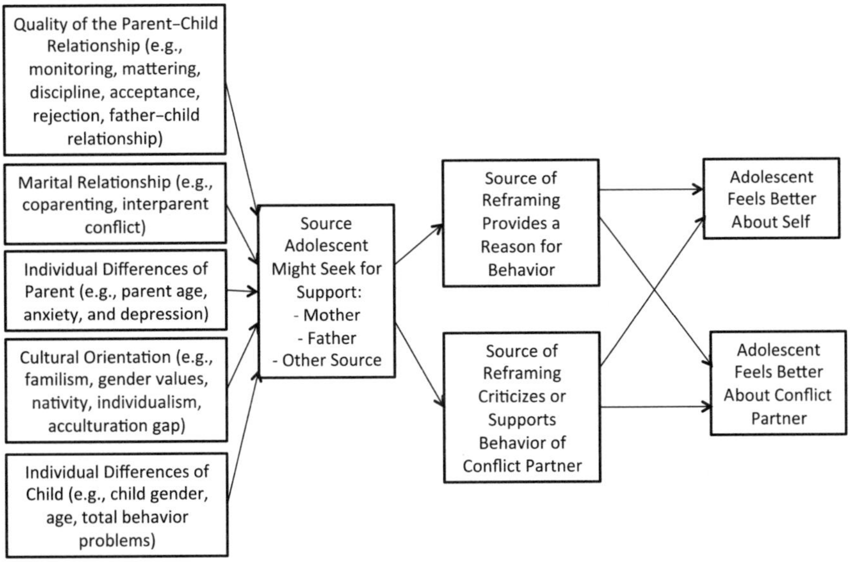

response to conflict that relies on social support and assists adolescents in reinterpreting or reappraising conflict situations. However, it is likely that the cognitive experience of reframing will depend on who is sought to provide the information. In other work (Cookston et al., under review), we test the latter part of this conceptual model of cognitive reframing; and in the current chapter we focus on the left side of the model to instead examine who adolescents talk to about father–adolescent conflict and specifically test the individual, family, and cultural-level factors that predict seeking out different sources. Next, we review whom adolescents turn to for support and the determinants of this support seeking.

Coping with Stress: To Whom Do Adolescents Turn?

Adolescents seek out different sources of social support over time and for different reasons. In middle childhood, parents tend to be the main sources of support for children; by the seventh grade, however, peers and parents play an approximately equal supportive role, and by tenth grade peers largely provide support (Furman & Buhrmester, 1992). During early adolescence, mothers still tend to be the primary confidants of youth (Nomaguchi, 2008; Reid, Landesman, Treder, & Jaccard, 1989). Nominated less often than mothers are fathers, peers, siblings, romantic partners (Nomaguchi, 2008), and adults outside of the family (Beam, Chen, & Greenberger, 2002). In addition to relying on parents less, the topics that parents and peers are sought out to support tend to be different, with peers sought for interpersonal issues and parents for school and career counseling (Youniss & Smollar, 1985). However, on average, adolescents tend to show worse functioning when they rely predominantly on their peers and not parents as confidants (Nomaguchi, 2008). One possible explanation for this is that peers appear to be more likely to defend the behavior of their age-mates rather than challenge one another towards changing behavior (Chen, Greenberger, Lester, Dong, & Guo, 1998). On the other hand, nonparent adult sources of support, also referred to as Very Important Persons (VIPs), may be well positioned to provide counsel to adolescents because they can offer support with the wisdom that adulthood provides (Chen, Greenberger, Farrugia, Bush & Dong, 2003) without seeming explicitly biased in favor of the parents (Greenberger, Chen, & Beam, 1998). According to our guided cognitive reframing model, a host of factors—individual, family, and cultural—will predict who adolescents seek out.

Individual, Family, and Cultural Predictors of Support Seeking

Although seeking support to discuss stressful events can be advantageous for youth, little is known about how adolescents decide whom to talk with and why certain confidants are sought for consultation or support. A number of individual and family-level qualities have been linked to whether adolescents are more likely to seek out parents or peers. At the individual level, younger adolescents (12–14-year-olds) tend to seek their parents more often than do older (15–17-year-olds) adolescents (Nomaguchi, 2008); similarly, females rely on parents more than do males (Windle, Miller-Tutzauer, Barnes, & Welte, 1991). Additionally, adolescents who demonstrate more risk behavior are less likely to report parents as confidants compared with those who show fewer risk behaviors (Nomaguchi, 2008). Transactional views of human development (Sameroff, 2010) suggest that younger adolescents, females, and adolescents with fewer problem behaviors might seek out their parents for support, providing evidence of the vital role adolescents play in shaping their own development.

In addition to qualities of the adolescent, existing research among primarily European American families suggests that parent–adolescent relationships and family structure are associated with use of parents as confidants. Adolescents who report better quality parent–adolescent relationships tend to seek their parents out more often as confidants than those who report lower quality relationships (Freeman & Brown, 2001), and children in married families tend to consult more with their parents than children in divorced families (Hetherington & Clingempeel, 1992). Given that parent–child relationships may be poorer in stepfamilies than intact families (Coleman & Ganong, 1997), one would expect lower levels of consultation with parents in stepfamilies than in intact families. In support of this expectation, adolescents in stepfamilies confide less in both mothers and fathers than adolescents in intact families (Dunn, Davies, O'Connor, & Sturgess, 2001). It is also likely that families experiencing high levels of interparental conflict may indirectly discourage children from discussing their own concerns with one parent for fear that it may cause more conflict between the parents (Buchanan, Maccoby, & Dornbusch, 1991).

In addition to individual and family-level factors, according to our guided cognitive reframing model, the cultural context may promote or discourage adolescents from seeking counsel about their parents' behaviors. If socialization goals place an emphasis on values of accepting authority, promoting interpersonal harmony, or striving for group success, seeking counsel about conflict with an authority figure may be considered disrespectful and, thus, may be discouraged (Hofstede, 1991). Adolescents in Mexican American families are encouraged to be respectful of authority figures (Keefe & Padilla, 1987), which might explain why Mexican American adolescents feel they are prevented from engaging in open communication about their parents' behavior (Cooper, Baker, Polichar, & Welsh, 1993). For example, Mexican American children show less eye contact with their parents than do European American children, presumably as a sign of respect for parental authority (Schofield, Castenada, Parke, & Coltrane, 2008).

However, individuals differ in their respective rates of acculturation to a host culture, exposure to socialization of traditional cultural values, and adherence to traditional family values; therefore, to understand confidant support requires attention to within-culture individual differences. For instance, when Mexican American adolescents show a more familistic orientation they also tend to use more active and solution-oriented conflict strategies for conflict resolution, regardless of whether the conflict partner was a sibling (Killoren, Thayer, & Updegraff, 2008) or friend (Thayer, Updegraff, & Delgado, 2008). In this case, it appears that the internalization of the cultural value of placing the family above the individual is associated with a behavioral approach to managing conflict. The findings of Killoren et al. (2008) and Thayer et al. (2008) portray Mexican American adolescents as active in conflict resolution and seem to contradict the Schofield et al. (2008) finding that Mexican American adolescents are less likely to use direct eye contact with their parents. Rather it is possible that expressions of conflict behavior may differ based on the adolescent's relationship to the conflict partner (sibling vs. parent), thus, having different cultural meanings and consequences for how conflict is resolved within families. These questions are, therefore, worthy of further study.

In the current chapter, we begin to fill the lacuna between the benefits of seeking others for support and the sparse evidence regarding how individual, family, and cultural factors explain seeking sources of social support. Specifically, we examined a series of constructs as predictors of whether mothers, resident fathers/stepfathers, and/or other sources were sought out as confidants by adolescents to discuss conflict with the resident father/stepfather. Although the father is only one of many possible conflict agents, the father is an appropriate target for initial consideration because mother–child relationships tend to be more consistent and culturally mandated (Leite & McKenry, 2002). By comparison, father–child relationships tend to be more variable in terms of the quality of the relationships as well as the quantity of time fathers spend with their children. Further, fathering tends to be less culturally prescribed, especially for stepfathers, relative to mothers. Thus, adolescents might seek support about fathers (especially stepfathers) because they are actively trying to make sense of those relationships. For the purposes of this chapter, "fathers" refer to the coresident men who, in our sample, are either biological fathers or stepfathers. Because our sample is diverse in terms of family structure and ethnicity, we give close consideration to these two family demographic characteristics in our analyses and the discussion of our findings.

An Analysis of Cultural Context and Seeking Support to Understand Conflict with Fathers

To predict how often adolescents reported seeking support from their mothers, fathers, and other sources we used characteristics of parents, marital relations, parenting, and family demographics as predictors, and we drew on a sample of 392 families. Our sample (see Schenck et al., 2009, for a description of the sample and Leidy et al., 2011, for information on measures and constructs) included seventh-grade adolescents (M age = 12.5, SD = .59, 52.3% female), and was approximately evenly divided between families of Mexican (49%) and European ancestry and between stepfather (44.5%) and biological father families. Of the Mexican American families, most of the mothers (64%) and fathers (68%) were born in Mexico, compared with only 19% of adolescents.

Assessment of the Source of Support. Within a longer interview, adolescents were asked to provide yes/no responses to the following question about their residential father, "When you are upset with your (dad/step-dad) or about your relationship with him, do you ever talk to . . .": (1) mom, (2) coresident dad/step-dad, and (3) anyone else. The responses to these questions served as our three dichotomous dependent variables.

Predictors of Sources of Support. To predict whether adolescents sought out their mother, father, and other sources, we relied on a number of constructs that accounted for aspects of the parent–adolescent relationship, marital relationship, parent and adolescent adjustment, the cultural context, and family demographics.

For our parent–adolescent relationship constructs we relied on composites of *monitoring of adolescent behavior* according to Stattin and Kerr's (2000) revised interpretation of (1) mother monitoring (r = .18 for mother and adolescent report) and (2) father monitoring (r = .31 for father and adolescent report). Quality of the parent–adolescent relationship with father was assessed with measures that included single-item indicators of (a) overall relationship with father (r = .47 for mother and adolescent report), and (b) adolescent reports of time spent with father. As described in Schenck et al. (2009), we also assessed a construct we refer to as *mattering* through separate constructs for adolescents' perceptions of the extent to which they were important figures in the lives of their mothers and fathers (separately).

To assess characteristics of the marital relationship, we created composites between combinations of mother, father, and adolescent reports of (1) marital conflict from the Children's Perceptions of Interparental Conflict Scale (Grych, Seid, & Fincham, 1992; composite of mother, father, and adolescent report, r = .57 for mother and father report, r = .42 for mother and adolescent report, r = .36 for father and adolescent report), and (2) coparenting from a 13-item measure of coparenting (Dumka & Roosa, 1995; r = .38 for mother and father report).

For parent behavior, we gathered information on mothers and fathers/stepfathers using adolescent reports from the Children's Report of Parent Behavior Inventory (Schaefer, 1965) of mother and father acceptance (α = .87 for mothers and .88 for fathers, 10 items), consistent discipline

(α = .71 for mothers and .71 for fathers, 8 items), and rejection (α = .81 for mothers and .79 for fathers, 10 items).

To assess individual differences among parents, parent-level constructs were created for mother and father psychopathology based on composites of mother report of anxiety and depression (r = .78) and father report of anxiety and depression (r = .68) from the Hopkins Symptom Checklist (Derogatis, 1974). Mothers and fathers also self-reported their age.

To assess information about cultural orientation, we used items from the Mexican American Cultural Values Scale (Knight et al., 2010) and created scores for (1) parent reports of familism (r = .35 for composite of mother and father report), (2) gender values (composite of mother, father, and adolescent report, r = .29 for mother and father report, r = .19 for mother and adolescent report, r = .23 for father and adolescent report), (3) parent endorsement of individualistic values (r = .31 for mother and father report), (4) adolescent endorsement of individualistic values, (5) parent–adolescent acculturation gap (i.e., the difference between parent and adolescent individualistic values), and (6) an interaction between adolescent and parent individualistic values. Additionally, we assessed whether mothers and fathers were born in Mexico.

Adolescent characteristics assessed included gender (1 = male, 2 = female; 52.3% of the sample was female), adolescent age (M = 12.5, SD = .59), and a composite of mother and father reports of the adolescent's total behavior problems using the Behavior Problem Inventory (Peterson & Zill, 1986; r = .47 for mother and father report).

Our analyses involved a two-step process. First, within the full sample of 392 families (and also separately by ethnic group) we estimated bivariate relations between each of the constructs in our model (see Table 5.1). Second, for each of the statistically significant bivariate associations, we conducted logistic regression models to separately predict whether mothers, fathers, and other sources were sought out, exploring whether ethnicity moderated these predictions. This method of forced entry of constructs based on bivariate associations reduces capitalizing on chance and overestimating confidence intervals (Cohen, Cohen, West, & Aiken, 2003).

Bivariate Associations. Our bivariate associations appear in Table 5.1 with European American (EA) families above the diagonal and Mexican American (MA) families below the diagonal.

Mothers. Adolescents more frequently sought out mother as a source of support when mothers monitored more, adolescents felt they mattered more to both parents, mother and father acceptance was high, mother rejection was low, and when fathers were older. None of the indices of cultural orientation related to seeking out mother.

Fathers. Adolescents more frequently sought out father as a source of support when parents monitored more, adolescents felt they mattered more to both parents, coparenting was higher, interparental conflict was

Table 5.1. Correlations Among Reframing, Parent Relationship and Behaviors, Acculturative Processes and Demographics

	1	2	3	4	5	6	7	8	9	10	11	12	13
1. Seek out mother (0 = no, 1 = yes)	1.00	0.28	0.01	−0.05	−0.15	0.02	0.03	−0.07	−0.10	−0.07	−0.06	−0.26	0.00
2. Seek out father (0 = no, 1 = yes)	0.29	1.00	−0.02	−0.27	−0.23	−0.12	0.09	−0.08	−0.21	0.09	−0.11	−0.16	−0.11
3. Seek out other (0 = no, 1 = yes)	0.05	−0.09	1.00	0.18	0.16	0.23	0.17	0.15	0.22	−0.14	0.13	0.22	0.14
4. Father monitoring (D, A)	0.11	0.28	−0.02	1.00	0.41	0.55	0.09	0.14	0.57	−0.15	0.38	0.13	0.24
5. Mother monitoring (M, A)	0.19	0.16	0.04	0.48	1.00	0.41	0.55	0.09	0.14	0.57	−0.15	0.38	0.13
6. Relationship with father (M, A)	0.07	0.28	−0.10	0.43	0.31	1.00	0.22	0.09	0.54	−0.32	0.56	0.17	0.25
7. Time spent with father (A)	0.16	0.05	0.01	0.15	0.17	0.26	1.00	0.01	0.14	−0.13	0.20	0.16	0.15
8. Mattering to mother (A)	0.19	0.11	0.02	0.26	0.33	0.20	0.11	1.00	0.39	−0.18	0.10	0.49	0.40
9. Mattering to father (A)	0.09	0.19	0.00	0.55	0.45	0.53	0.22	0.46	1.00	−0.21	0.33	0.22	0.29
10. Interparental conflict (M, D, A)	−0.18	−0.25	0.10	−0.15	−0.17	−0.32	−0.03	−0.05	−0.12	1.00	−0.38	−0.12	−0.36
11. Coparenting (M, D)	0.15	0.15	−0.01	0.31	0.23	0.51	0.12	0.15	0.27	−0.38	1.00	0.09	0.28
12. Mother acceptance (A)	0.30	0.28	−0.02	0.28	0.39	0.17	0.14	0.60	0.38	−0.16	0.15	1.00	0.18
13. Mother discipline (A)	−0.01	0.05	−0.07	0.25	0.37	0.11	0.05	0.33	0.35	−0.05	0.06	0.18	1.00
14. Mom rejection (A)	−0.12	−0.11	0.06	−0.38	−0.48	−0.13	−0.10	−0.54	−0.44	0.14	−0.06	−0.46	−0.65
15. Father acceptance (A)	0.19	0.38	−0.03	0.53	0.40	0.61	0.22	0.28	0.66	−0.20	0.36	0.55	0.13
16. Father discipline (A)	0.00	−0.02	−0.07	0.24	0.31	0.28	0.15	0.19	0.36	−0.13	0.06	0.08	0.65
17. Father rejection (A)	−0.06	−0.16	0.14	−0.31	−0.35	−0.46	−0.27	−0.14	−0.49	0.17	−0.05	−0.16	−0.44
18. Mother anxiety & depression (M)	−0.08	−0.13	0.03	−0.07	−0.22	−0.29	−0.09	−0.08	−0.15	0.24	−0.30	0.00	−0.04
19. Father anxiety & depression (D)	0.03	−0.02	−0.07	−0.08	−0.01	−0.06	0.01	−0.02	0.00	0.22	−0.36	−0.08	0.12
20. Familism (M, D)	0.04	0.02	−0.04	−0.06	0.24	0.04	0.07	0.02	−0.06	−0.15	0.24	0.00	0.07
21. Gender values (M, D, A)	0.02	0.00	−0.08	−0.06	0.10	0.01	−0.01	0.00	−0.08	−0.05	0.13	0.01	0.00
22. Parent individualism (M, D)	−0.01	0.01	−0.09	−0.10	0.13	−0.06	−0.12	−0.03	−0.13	−0.12	0.07	0.02	0.00
23. Adolescent individualism (A)	−0.02	−0.06	0.10	0.07	−0.02	0.06	−0.07	0.09	0.04	0.00	−0.04	0.04	−0.23
24. Individualism gap ([M+D/2]−A)	−0.02	−0.04	0.02	0.13	−0.11	0.10	0.03	0.10	0.12	0.08	−0.08	0.02	−0.18
25. Parent by child individualism	0.01	−0.05	0.13	0.02	0.07	0.01	−0.11	0.06	−0.03	−0.06	0.01	0.05	−0.14
26. Mother born in Mexico (M)	−0.03	−0.08	0.12	0.10	0.16	−0.10	−0.07	0.12	0.05	−0.08	0.12	0.11	0.19
27. Father born in Mexico (D)	−0.08	−0.10	0.18	−0.01	0.09	−0.19	−0.04	−0.03	−0.11	−0.10	0.02	0.13	−0.01
28. Child behavior problems (M, D)	−0.02	−0.21	−0.09	−0.31	−0.33	−0.28	−0.07	−0.19	−0.30	0.09	−0.23	−0.09	−0.20
29. Child gender (male = 1; female = 2)	0.03	0.00	0.22	0.07	0.28	0.11	−0.04	0.19	0.19	0.03	0.17	0.08	0.20
30. Mother age (M)	−0.08	0.06	0.05	−0.02	0.03	0.02	0.05	0.06	0.09	−0.10	0.06	0.04	0.06
31. Father age (D)	−0.11	−0.07	0.07	0.16	0.13	0.13	0.16	0.12	0.21	−0.10	0.12	0.16	0.19
32. Child age (A)	−0.07	−0.01	−0.05	−0.12	−0.18	0.04	0.01	−0.12	−0.12	0.00	0.04	−0.15	−0.10
33. Father status (intact = 1; step = 2)	−0.04	0.03	−0.02	−0.29	−0.11	−0.16	−0.08	−0.06	−0.32	0.07	−0.18	−0.04	−0.14

Note. Listwise n = 180 European American (above diagonal), n = 183 Mexican origin (below diagonal); M = mother report, D = father report, A = adolescent report; Correlations are significant at p = .05 when r = .147, p = .01 at r = .190, p = .001 at r = .235.

NEW DIRECTIONS FOR CHILD AND ADOLESCENT DEVELOPMENT • DOI: 10.1002/cd

Table 5.1. (continued) Correlations Among Reframing, Parent Relationship and Behaviors, Acculturative Processes and Demographics

	14	15	16	17	18	19	20	21	22	23	24	25	26
1. Seek out mother (0 = no, 1 = yes)	0.10	-0.11	0.08	0.03	0.04	0.09	0.08	0.13	0.08	0.03	-0.02	0.08	—
2. Seek out father (0 = no, 1 = yes)	0.09	-0.29	-0.09	0.18	-0.02	0.08	-0.12	-0.02	-0.01	0.07	0.07	0.06	—
3. Seek out other (0 = no, 1 = yes)	-0.15	0.27	0.17	-0.21	-0.15	-0.02	-0.09	-0.02	-0.02	-0.01	0.00	-0.02	—
4. Father monitoring (D, A)	-0.18	0.57	0.31	-0.36	-0.19	-0.29	0.14	-0.03	-0.06	0.03	0.06	-0.01	—
5. Mother monitoring (M, A)	0.24	-0.18	0.57	0.31	-0.36	-0.19	0.04	0.14	-0.03	-0.09	-0.03	-0.12	—
6. Relationship with father (M, A)	-0.16	0.66	0.34	-0.51	-0.27	-0.32	0.09	0.06	-0.10	-0.02	0.04	-0.07	—
7. Time spent with father (A)	-0.08	0.16	0.12	-0.14	-0.09	-0.10	0.08	0.19	-0.01	0.13	0.12	0.09	—
8. Mattering to mother (A)	-0.54	0.14	0.27	-0.30	-0.04	-0.16	-0.13	-0.11	-0.08	0.04	0.09	-0.02	—
9. Mattering to father (A)	-0.27	0.66	0.41	-0.57	-0.11	-0.25	0.14	0.02	-0.19	-0.01	0.11	-0.11	—
10. Interparental conflict (M, D, A)	0.24	-0.24	-0.34	0.29	0.42	0.42	0.03	-0.01	-0.28	0.04	-0.14	0.19	—
11. Coparenting (M, D)	-0.18	0.33	0.26	-0.35	-0.46	-0.39	0.10	0.00	-0.28	-0.03	0.15	-0.17	—
12. Mother acceptance (A)	-0.49	0.38	0.19	-0.23	0.00	-0.08	-0.03	-0.02	0.01	0.08	0.07	0.07	—
13. Mother discipline (A)	-0.67	0.24	0.53	-0.53	-0.18	-0.14	0.15	0.12	-0.23	-0.06	0.09	-0.18	—
14. Mom rejection (A)	1.00	-0.21	-0.40	0.59	0.11	0.11	-0.01	0.01	0.18	0.18	0.04	0.24	—
15. Father acceptance (A)	-0.27	1.00	0.28	-0.50	-0.10	-0.22	0.12	0.05	-0.08	0.06	0.11	0.00	—
16. Father discipline (A)	-0.55	0.15	1.00	-0.59	-0.24	-0.16	0.08	-0.04	-0.16	-0.08	0.03	-0.15	—
17. Father rejection (A)	0.55	-0.46	-0.59	1.00	0.24	0.22	-0.07	-0.02	0.16	0.10	-0.01	0.17	—
18. Mother anxiety & depression (M)	0.05	-0.13	-0.05	0.06	1.00	0.26	0.01	0.09	0.14	0.04	-0.05	0.11	—
19. Father anxiety & depression (D)	-0.06	-0.02	0.13	-0.12	0.16	1.00	-0.09	-0.08	0.12	0.03	-0.05	0.09	—
20. Familism (M, D)	-0.03	0.01	-0.02	-0.02	0.01	-0.12	1.00	0.67	0.17	0.03	-0.08	0.12	—
21. Gender values (M, D, A)	0.03	0.02	-0.07	0.04	0.04	-0.14	0.68	1.00	0.08	0.08	0.02	0.10	—
22. Parent individualism (M, D)	-0.05	-0.06	-0.05	0.04	0.05	-0.02	0.67	0.57	1.00	0.18	-0.47	0.68	—
23. Adolescent individualism (A)	0.14	0.11	-0.14	0.10	0.13	0.06	0.08	0.06	0.13	1.00	0.78	0.84	—
24. Individualism gap ([M+D/2]-A)	0.15	0.13	-0.08	0.05	0.07	0.07	-0.41	-0.35	-0.59	0.72	1.00	0.32	—
25. Parent by child individualism	0.06	0.05	-0.11	0.09	0.13	0.04	0.45	0.39	0.69	0.80	0.17	1.00	—
26. Mother born in Mexico (M)	-0.22	0.05	0.06	-0.10	0.00	0.07	0.36	0.17	0.39	0.10	-0.19	0.31	1.00
27. Father born in Mexico (D)	-0.09	-0.02	-0.06	-0.03	0.09	-0.09	0.30	0.20	0.43	-0.02	-0.31	0.25	0.59
28. Child behavior problems (M, D)	0.24	-0.19	-0.10	0.20	0.30	0.18	-0.07	-0.05	0.00	0.18	0.14	0.13	-0.14
29. Child gender (male = 1; female = 2)	-0.17	0.10	0.26	-0.24	-0.09	0.01	0.02	0.00	-0.02	-0.04	-0.02	-0.04	0.13
30. Mother age (M)	-0.12	-0.08	0.11	-0.02	0.03	0.00	-0.03	0.01	0.01	0.02	0.01	0.02	0.03
31. Father age (D)	-0.21	0.10	0.19	-0.12	-0.08	0.06	-0.06	-0.07	-0.04	0.01	0.03	0.02	0.03
32. Child age (A)	0.24	-0.12	-0.02	0.13	0.03	-0.01	0.00	0.00	-0.04	-0.04	0.00	-0.02	0.09
33. Father status (intact = 1; step = 2)	0.15	-0.14	-0.07	0.05	0.07	0.06	-0.04	-0.06	-0.05	0.03	0.05	-0.01	-0.16

Note: Listwise $n = 180$ European American (above diagonal), $n = 183$ Mexican origin (below diagonal); M = mother report, D = father report, A = adolescent report; Correlations are significant at $p = .05$ when $r = .147$, $p = .01$ at $r = .190$, $p = .001$ at $r = .235$.

Table 5.1. (continued) Correlations Among Reframing, Parent Relationship and Behaviors, Acculturative Processes and Demographics

	27	28	29	30	31	32	33
1. Seek out mother (0 = no, 1 = yes)	—	0.07	−0.09	−0.07	−0.11	0.02	0.04
2. Seek out father (0 = no, 1 = yes)	—	0.11	−0.06	−0.09	0.01	−0.02	0.26
3. Seek out other (0 = no, 1 = yes)	—	−0.05	−0.14	−0.01	−0.03	−0.03	−0.15
4. Father monitoring (D, A)	—	−0.34	0.11	0.00	0.04	−0.17	−0.30
5. Mother monitoring (M, A)	—	−0.01	−0.34	0.15	0.17	0.11	−0.17
6. Relationship with father (M, A)	—	−0.43	0.12	−0.05	−0.03	−0.17	−0.19
7. Time spent with father (A)	—	0.03	0.04	0.00	−0.02	−0.05	−0.02
8. Mattering to mother (A)	—	−0.12	−0.01	−0.01	−0.01	−0.01	0.03
9. Mattering to father (A)	—	−0.24	0.14	0.04	0.13	−0.22	−0.34
10. Interparental conflict (M, D, A)	—	0.27	−0.05	−0.14	−0.01	0.05	0.17
11. Coparenting (M, D)	—	−0.38	0.09	0.06	0.00	−0.06	−0.20
12. Mother acceptance (A)	—	−0.08	0.03	−0.05	−0.10	−0.03	0.02
13. Mother discipline (A)	—	−0.31	0.01	0.12	0.12	−0.07	−0.26
14. Mom rejection (A)	—	0.28	−0.05	−0.03	−0.04	0.07	0.20
15. Father acceptance (A)	—	−0.24	0.08	0.02	0.03	−0.22	−0.27
16. Father discipline (A)	—	−0.28	0.03	0.05	0.07	−0.15	−0.21
17. Father rejection (A)	—	0.27	−0.10	−0.01	−0.11	0.18	0.25
18. Mother anxiety & depression (M)	—	0.42	−0.04	−0.21	−0.05	0.06	0.12
19. Father anxiety & depression (D)	—	0.31	−0.13	−0.08	−0.06	−0.03	−0.01
20. Familism (M, D)	—	−0.11	−0.02	−0.13	−0.09	−0.08	−0.12
21. Gender values (M, D, A)	—	0.00	−0.01	0.01	−0.04	0.02	−0.08
22. Parent individualism (M, D)	—	−0.17	0.00	−0.07	−0.04	0.05	0.19
23. Adolescent individualism(A)	—	0.11	−0.12	0.00	0.01	0.08	0.13
24. Individualism gap ([M+D/2]−A)	—	−0.01	−0.11	0.04	0.04	0.04	−0.01
25. Parent by child individualism	—	0.18	−0.10	−0.04	−0.02	0.08	0.20
26. Mother born in Mexico (M)	—	—	—	—	—	—	—
27. Father born in Mexico (D)	1.00	—	—	—	—	—	—
28. Child behavior problems (M, D)	−0.05	1.00	−0.10	−0.06	−0.05	0.11	0.16
29. Child gender (male = 1; female = 2)	0.00	−0.16	1.00	0.02	−0.02	−0.20	0.05
30. Mother age (M)	−0.03	−0.07	−0.03	1.00	0.58	−0.05	−0.29
31. Father age (D)	0.04	−0.12	0.01	0.68	1.00	−0.06	−0.21
32. Child age (A)	−0.16	0.03	−0.14	0.01	0.02	1.00	0.08
33. Father status (intact = 1; step = 2)	−0.10	0.19	0.00	−0.33	−0.29	0.11	1.00

Note: Listwise $n = 180$ European American (above diagonal), $n = 183$ Mexican origin (below diagonal); M = mother report; D = father report, A = adolescent report; Correlations are significant at $p = .05$ when $r = .147$, $p = .01$ at $r = .190$, $p = .001$ at $r = .235$.

lower (and this association differed by ethnicity with $r = -.08$, $p = .26$ for EA and $r = -.23$, $p = .001$ for MA adolescents), and the quality of the relationship with father was higher. Additionally, five of the six parenting behaviors were associated with seeking the father (only father discipline was not related). Also linked to seeking father as a source of support were higher levels of mother and father acceptance, lower levels of mother and father rejection, and higher mother consistent discipline. One element of the adolescent was linked with seeking out father for reframing: lower levels of adolescent behavior problems. Also, adolescents in intact families ($\chi^2 = 6.833$, $p = .009$) and European American families were more likely to seek out father support ($\chi^2 = 6.41$, $p = .011$) than adolescents in either stepfather families or in Mexican American households. No indices of cultural orientation were related to reports of seeking out father.

Other Sources. Adolescents sought other sources more when parents monitored less, the overall relationship with father was low, time shared with the father was low ($r = .19$, $p = .005$ for EA and $r = .02$, $p = .82$ for MA adolescents), and the adolescent reported low levels of mattering to the father ($r = -.21$, $p = .003$ for EA and $r = .01$, $p = .881$ for MA adolescents) and mother ($r = -.15$, $p = .035$ for EA and $r = .02$, $p = .774$ for MA adolescents). At the adolescent level, more adolescent anxiety and depression was associated with seeking other sources. With respect to the marital relationship, higher levels of interparental conflict were related to seeking out other sources. When all six parenting behaviors were less adaptive, other sources were sought more often: low mother and father acceptance, low mother and father discipline, and high levels of mother and father rejection. Also, boys were less likely than girls to seek out another source ($\chi^2 = 13.89$, $p < .001$). Seeking out other sources was associated with only one indicator of cultural orientation; among the Mexican American adolescents, other sources were sought more often when either the mother or father was born in Mexico.

Logistic Regression. In our final analysis, we sought to understand which of the individual and family-level constructs predicted who was sought out to discuss conflict with fathers. Rather than predict each of our dependent variables separately, we estimated a multiple group path analysis logistic regression model in Mplus v6.1 (Muthén & Muthén, 2010). Such an analysis is parsimonious because it allows for the estimation of a single model (vs. three separate models) and accounts for the relations among the three dependent variables. Although data-driven, we dropped predictors of each dependent variable from the final model if the construct was not associated at the bivariate level for the full sample at $p < .01$, or at $p < .05$ for either ethnicity group. For paths that appeared to operate differently for the adolescents of Mexican and European ancestry, we allowed the path between a predictor and outcome to vary for the two groups to address the moderating role of ethnicity. When the difference in an association appeared to be negligible, we fixed the path to be equal between groups. Differences in chi-square estimates for the models were explored before accepting the final model.

Fit was adequate in the final model (χ^2 = 71.65, df = 77, p = .42, Weighted Root Mean Square Residual = 1.096). We were able to fix the association between the two ethnicities for associations among the dependent variables. Results showed seeking out mother was associated with seeking out father (b = .53, p < .001), but seeking the other source was unrelated to seeking father (r = .02, p = .835) or mother (r = −.14, p = .108). It is not surprising that the participants in our sample who sought out one parent also tended to seek out the other parent; however, it was unclear why seeking parents and other sources was unrelated.

Mother. In predicting seeking out mother, we included coparenting, mattering to mother and father, paternal age, maternal monitoring, maternal acceptance and rejection, and paternal acceptance (see Figure 5.2 for final model). For all seven constructs, we were able to fix the paths between the two ethnic groups suggesting common patterns between the two groups. When the block of predictors was included, coparenting and maternal acceptance were the two constructs that predicted seeking mother such that higher coparenting—the perception that parents work together as a team—and more maternal acceptance were associated with seeking out mothers. In the case of acceptance, adolescents may seek their mother when she can provide support and likely will not seek the mother when the adolescent perceives the parents do not agree on parenting strategies as in the case of low coparenting. These results further demonstrate the links between parent characteristics, marital processes, and support that have been observed within families of young children (Stright & Bales, 2003), and our findings extend these associations to adolescence.

Father. In predicting seeking out father, we included coparenting and interparental conflict, maternal and paternal monitoring, adolescent behavior problems, overall relationship with father, stepfamily status, mattering to mother and father, mother acceptance and rejection, and father acceptance. In the final model, we allowed separate paths between ethnic groups for only interparental conflict. For Mexican American families only, lower interparental conflict was associated with seeking out father. For both ethnic groups, higher levels of father monitoring and acceptance predicted seeking out father. It appears that like mothers, the father's acceptance level explains whether adolescents seek him out. Furthermore, that father monitoring is linked to seeking out father provides support for the notion that parental monitoring is adolescent-directed through disclosure on behalf of the adolescent (Kerr, Stattin, & Pakaliniskiene, 2008).

Other Sources. In predicting seeking out other sources, we included interparental conflict, maternal and paternal monitoring, overall relationship with father, time spent with father, adolescent gender, mattering to mother and father, and mother and father acceptance, rejection, and discipline. Although significant at the bivariate level among the Mexican

Figure 5.2. Unstandardized estimates for significant predictors of whether mothers, coresident fathers/stepfathers, and anyone else were sought out to discuss conflict with a coresident father

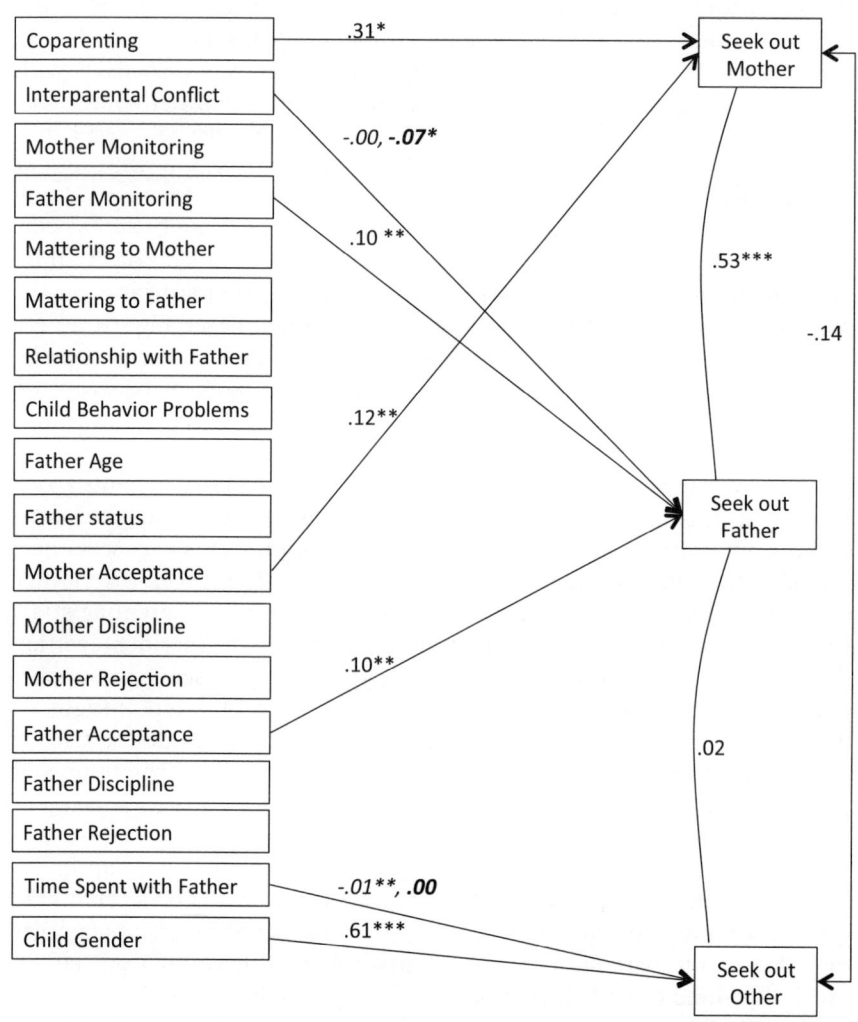

Predictor	→ Seek out Mother	→ Seek out Father	→ Seek out Other
Coparenting	.31*		
Interparental Conflict			
Mother Monitoring	-.00, *-.07**		
Father Monitoring		.10**	
Mattering to Mother			
Mattering to Father			
Relationship with Father			
Child Behavior Problems		.12**	
Father Age			
Father status			
Mother Acceptance			
Mother Discipline			
Mother Rejection		.10**	
Father Acceptance			
Father Discipline			
Father Rejection			
Time Spent with Father		*-.01*** , **.00**	
Child Gender			.61***

Correlations: Seek out Mother ↔ Seek out Father: .53***; Seek out Mother ↔ Seek out Other: -.14; Seek out Father ↔ Seek out Other: .02

Note: Child gender: male = 1, female = 2; Father status: intact family = 1, stepfather = 2; Paths with single values were fixed between Mexican American (MA) and European American (EA) families. Paths with two numbers report differences between groups where italicized values are for the EA families and bold values are from the MA subgroup.
*p < .05. **p < .01. ***p < .001.

American families, parent nativity was not included in the logistic regression because it was a constant for the European American families (i.e., all were born in the United States). Of the 14 paths predicting seeking the other source, 6 were estimated separately for the two groups (maternal and paternal monitoring, time spent with father, mattering to mother, and mother and father acceptance). Consistent with past research (Windle et al., 1991), among both ethnic groups, girls were more likely to seek another source than were boys. Estimated separately for the two ethnic groups, time spent with father was unrelated to seeking out other sources among the Mexican American families, while less time spent with father was associated with seeking out other sources in the European American families.

Predictors of Sources of Support Sought: A Summary. Because father–adolescent relationships tend to be more variable than mother–adolescent relationships, adolescents may require more support in navigating this important family relationship; however, seeking support about conflict with father is clearly situated within qualities of the family context. Our results compliment past evidence on the experience of young adolescents by demonstrating that the adaptive behavior of seeking out parents to reframe conflict with father is associated with qualities of the parent (i.e., accepting parenting, monitoring) and qualities of the family context (i.e., interparental conflict and coparenting). For example, mothers were sought out when they were more accepting and fathers were sought out more when they were involved in monitoring the adolescent's behavior. Although girls were more likely to report seeking other sources, gender was not important in explaining whether mothers and fathers were sought.

We also found that ethnicity did not add considerable variability to the patterns of seeking out sources of support among adolescents (only 8 of 30 paths demonstrated significantly different patterns of association and many of these were negligible). Rather, the links between parenting and family context were approximately equal for the two ethnicities suggesting the normative and common nature of these processes between groups. As we have demonstrated by comparing the extant literature and evidence from families of Mexican American and European American origin, there was a compelling trend in favor of common processes associated with patterns of seeking out sources of support. Qualities of the parents themselves (i.e., monitoring for fathers and acceptance for both parents) explained whether they were sought out. Furthermore, adolescents tended to seek mothers more when levels of coparenting were higher, possibly to avoid creating further conflict in the interparental relationship. Surprisingly, where prior research on the cultural traditions of Mexican American families has emphasized elements of heightened familism and deference to parental authority, our results suggested these patterns were unrelated to seeking out father or father-figures as confidants. In the results we have reported here, the only differential link between ethnicity and support seeking occurred for seeking out fathers and interparental conflict. Mexican American (but not the European American) adolescents were less likely to seek father when conflict levels were high. Our analyses and review of the literature suggest that cultural factors played a less important role in seeking out mothers, fathers, and other sources for support. Rather, when parents tended to be accepting, adolescents would seek them out, suggesting the important transactional nature of parent–adolescent relationships.

These findings support many aspects of the guided cognitive reframing model, namely, the factors that influence the targets chosen by adolescents for support in the face of conflict. In support of an active coping strategy interpretation of guided cognitive reframing, the empirical results we reported suggest adolescents select parents for reframing based on qualities of the adolescent, parent–adolescent relationship, and family context. Specifically, both mothers and fathers are selected when they are more accepting of the adolescent. Fathers, on the other hand, are also sought when adolescents already tend to disclose information to them. Clearly, adolescents seek parents when those sources tend to be open to conversations about parent–adolescent relationships. Additionally, in terms of the family context, mothers are also sought when parents tend to agree in their parenting strategies. However, while we found support for whom adolescents seek out to provide counsel and why they chose those sources, the fact that the cultural variables did not play a significant role in this process suggests an important direction for future research to examine.

Conclusions and Future Directions

The current review and analyses highlight the factors that influence whether sources are sought for guided cognitive reframing; however, there are a number of topics that require further consideration. First, virtually nothing is known about the social context of guided cognitive reframing in the lives of adolescents. Regular conversations about sexual health and behavior with parents tend to make future conversations easier (Coffelt, 2010); however, it is unclear whether daily negotiations of social support seeking in families work similarly. The results we provided suggest that a history of open communication between parents likely is associated with parents being sought for conversations about conflict with the father. Rather than social support occurring on a daily basis, it is possible that social support is negotiated on an instance-by-instance basis with support sought at the time of a conflict. Alternatively, social support may be sought only after a number of conflict situations have occurred. Future research should attempt to understand how frequently support is sought as a function of the regularity of conflict. Second, it will be important to explore whether certain conflict topics are more likely to result in seeking support while others are less likely. Consider, for example, the distinction between the everyday conflict that occurs within families and the acculturation-based conflict that occurs within immigrant families (Juang et al., this volume). An adolescent may be less likely to seek support to understand "everyday" sources of conflict from parents (e.g., conflict about clothing and chores) but may be more likely to seek out a peer. On the other hand, for acculturative conflict a different pattern may emerge because parents may acculturate at different rates given unique vocational demands (Parke, Vega, Cookston, Perez-Brena, & Coltrane, 2008). For example, if one parent works outside the home and the other does not, the parent who works outside the home may acculturate more quickly. Alternatively, if one parent works in a more ethnically homogeneous workplace, that parent may acculturate more slowly. It is, thus, possible that adolescents may be more likely to seek support regarding arguments with one parent about culturally prescribed behaviors and values as these values may vary by the acculturation of parents. Furthermore, support regarding culturally based conflict may be especially beneficial if reframed by another person who has a dual frame of reference (e.g., an older sibling who may be less acculturated, but has more experience with U.S. cultural norms than a parent).

It is also possible that multiple sources are sought out to assist with reframing the same conflict situation. After an argument with his mother over a family rule, a son might seek out the father to understand the reason for the mother's behavior, might ask the mother for an apology, and might ask whether a friend is subject to a similar rule. By seeking multiple sources to obtain unique perspectives on a common event, an adolescent might end up feeling better suited to face similar conflict situations in the future. While our results did not address whether different sources are sought, it does appear that similar qualities of parents, namely, accepting parenting, and healthier marital relationships may explain whether parents are sought. Relatedly, in addition to not addressing whether multiple sources were sought to address the same conflict event, a key limitation of the current analyses is that we did not address who the other sources were and what might explain going to different sources. In our earlier review we addressed how both peers and VIPs might be sought. It is likely that there are differences in individual, family, and cultural explanations for when sources are sought and this is an area that merits future study.

Finally, a theme that cuts across each of these areas of future study concerns the stability, function, and benefits of seeking support over time in the lives of adolescents. Just as adolescents make the transition to age-mates as confidants, it is also possible that sources of guided cognitive reframing are also changing regularly as friendships fade, as individuals prove to be unsatisfactory counsel, and as romantic relationships increase in importance for teens. Additionally, changes in decision-making during adolescence (Steinberg, 2010) may afford adolescents an opportunity to understand the benefits of seeking out sources for guided cognitive reframing as well as change the kind of information sought and the expected benefits of seeking support. As poet Elbert Hubbard noted, "We find what we expect to find, and we receive what we ask for" (Hubbard, 1922, p. 41), but further research on guided cognitive reframing may also make it possible to change what is expected and received.

References

Barber, J. G., & Delfabbro, P. (2000). Predictors of adolescent adjustment: Parent-peer relationships and parent-child conflict. *Child and Adolescent Social Work Journal, 17*(4), 275–288.

Beam, M., Chen, C., & Greenberger, E. (2002). The nature of adolescents' relationships with their 'very important' nonparental adults. *American Journal of Community Psychology, 30*(2), 305–325.

Buchanan, C. M., Maccoby, E. E., & Dornbusch, S. M. (1991). Caught between parents: Adolescents' experience in divorced homes. *Child Development, 62*(5), 1008–1029.

Chen, C., Greenberger, E., Farrugia, S., Bush, K., & Dong, Q. (2003). Beyond parents and peers: The role of important non-parental adults (VIPS) in adolescent development in China and the United States. *Psychology in the Schools, 40*, 35–50.

Chen, C., Greenberger, E., Lester, J., Dong, Q., & Guo, M. (1998). A cross-cultural study of family and peer correlates of adolescent misconduct. *Developmental Psychology, 34*(4), 770–781.

Chung, G., Flook, L., & Fuligni, A. (2009). Daily family conflict and emotional distress among adolescents from Latin American, Asian, and European backgrounds. *Developmental Psychology, 45*(5), 1406–1415.

Coffelt, T. A. (2010). Is sexual communication challenging between mothers and daughters? *Journal of Family Communication, 10*(2), 116–130.

Cohen, J., Cohen, P., West, S. G., & Aiken, L. S. (2003). *Applied multiple regression/correlation analyses for the behavioral sciences* (3rd ed.). Hillsdale, NJ: Erlbaum.

Coleman, M., & Ganong, L. H. (1997). Stepfamilies from the stepfamily's perspective. *Marriage and Family Review, 26*, 107–121.

Connor-Smith, J. K., Compas, B. E., Wadsworth, M. E., Thomsen, A. H., & Saltzman, H. (2000). Responses to stress in adolescence: Measurement of coping and involuntary stress responses. *Journal of Consulting and Clinical Psychology, 68*(6), 976–992.

Cookston, J. T., Olide, A. F., Braver, S. L., Fabricius, W. V., & Saenz, D. (under review). He said what! Guided cognitive reframing about the father-adolescent relationship. Manuscript submitted for publication.

Cooper, C. R., Baker, H., Polichar, D., & Welsh, M. (1993). Values and communication of Chinese, Filipino, European, Mexican, and Vietnamese American adolescents with their families and friends. In S. Shulman, A. W. Collins (Eds.), *Father–adolescent relationships* (pp. 73–89). San Francisco, CA: Jossey-Bass.

DeCarlo Santiago, C., & Wadsworth, M. E. (2009). Coping with family conflict: What's helpful and what's not for low-income adolescents. *Journal of Child and Family Studies, 18*(2), 192–202.

Derogatis, L. R. (1974) The Hopkins Symptom Checklist (HSCL): A self-report symptom inventory. *Behavioral-Science, 19*(1), 1–15.

Dumka, L. E., & Roosa, M. W. (1995). The role of stress and family relationships in mediating problem drinking and fathers' personal adjustment. *Journal of Studies on Alcohol, 56*(5), 528–537.

Dunn, J., Davies, L. C., O'Connor, T. G., & Sturgess, W. (2001). Family lives and friendships: The perspectives of children in step-, single-parent, and nonstep families. *Journal of Family Psychology, 15*(2), 272–287.
Freeman, H., & Brown, B. (2001). Primary attachment to parents and peers during adolescence: Differences by attachment style. *Journal of Youth and Adolescence, 30*(6), 653–674.
Furman, W., & Buhrmester, D. (1992). Age and sex differences in perceptions of networks of personal relationships. *Child Development, 63*(1), 103–115.
Gonzales, N., Deardorff, J., Formoso, D., Barr, A., & Barrera, M. (2006). Family mediators of the relation between acculturation and adolescent mental health. *Family Relations, 55*(3), 318–330.
Granic, I., Hollenstein, T., Dishion, T. J., & Patterson, G. R. (2003). Longitudinal analysis of flexibility and reorganization in early adolescence: A dynamic systems study of family interactions. *Developmental Psychology, 39*(3), 606–617.
Greenberger, E., Chen, C., & Beam, M. R. (1998). The role of 'very important' nonparental adults in adolescent development. *Journal of Youth and Adolescence, 27*(3), 321–343.
Grych, J. H., Seid, M., & Fincham, F. D. (1992). Assessing marital conflict from the child's perspective: The children's perception of interparental conflict scale. *Child Development, 63*, 558–572.
Hetherington, E., & Clingempeel, W. (1992). Coping with marital transitions: A family systems perspective. *Monographs of the Society for Research in Child Development, 57*(2–3), 1–242.
Hofstede, G. (1991). Empirical models of cultural differences. In N. Bliechrodt, P. D. Drenth (Eds.), *Contemporary issues in cross-cultural psychology* (pp. 4–20). Lisse Netherlands: Swets & Zeitlinger Publishers.
Hubbard, F. E. (1922). *The Elect: Elbert Hubbard's selected writings Part 5*. London, England: Roycrofters.
Juang, L. P., Syed, M., Cookston, J. T., Wang, Y., & Kim, S. Y. (2012). Acculturation-based and everyday family conflict in Chinese American Families. In L. P. Juang & A. J. Umaña-Taylor (Eds.), *Family conflict among Chinese- and Mexican-origin adolescents and their parents in the U.S. New Directions for Child and Adolescent Development, 135*, 13–34.
Keefe, S. E., & Padilla, A. M. (1987). *Chicano ethnicity*. Albuquerque, NM: University of New Mexico Press.
Kerr, M., Stattin, H., & Pakaliniskiene, V. (2008). Parents react to adolescent problem behaviors by worrying more and monitoring less. In M. Kerr, H. Stattin, & R. Engels (Eds.), *What can parents do?: New insights into the role of parents in adolescent problem behavior* (pp. 91–112). London, England: Wiley.
Killoren, S., Thayer, S., & Updegraff, K. (2008). Conflict resolution between Mexican origin adolescent siblings. *Journal of Marriage and Family, 70*(5), 1200–1212.
Knight, G. P., Gonzales, N. A., Saenz, D. S., Bonds, D. D., Germán, M., Deardorff, J., & Updegraff, K. A. (2010). The Mexican American Cultural Values Scale for adolescents and adults. *The Journal of Early Adolescence, 30*(3), 444–481.
Kovacs, M. (1992). *Children's Depression Inventory*. New York, NY: Multi-Health Systems, Inc.
Lazarus, R. S. (1991). *Emotion and Adaptation*. New York, NY: Oxford University Press.
Leidy, M., Schofield, T., Miller, M., Parke, R. D., Coltrane, S., Cookston, J., . . . Adams, M. (2011). Fathering and adolescent adjustment: Variations by family structure and ethnic background. *Fathering, 9*, 44–68.
Leite, R. W., & McKenry, P. C. (2002). Aspects of father status and postdivorce father involvement with children. *Journal of Family Issues, 23*(5), 601–623.
Muthén, L. K., & Muthén, B. O. (2010). *Mplus*. Los Angeles, CA: Muthén & Muthén.

Noguchi, K. (2008). Gender, family structure, and adolescents' primary confidants. *Journal of Marriage and Family, 70*(5), 1213–1227.

Ohannessian, C., Bradley, J., Waninger, K., Ruddy, K., Hepp, B., & Hesselbrock, V. (2010). An examination of adolescent coping typologies and young adult alcohol use in a high-risk sample. *Vulnerable Children and Youth Studies, 5*(1), 52–65.

Parke, R. D., Vega, E., Cookston, J. T., Perez-Brena, N., & Coltrane, S. (2008). Imagining the future of immigrant fathers. In S. S. Chuang & R. P. Moreno (Eds.), *On new shores: Understanding immigrant fathers in North America* (pp. 289–318). New York, NY: Lexington Books.

Peterson, J. L, & Zill, N. (1986). Marital disruption, parent-child relationships, and behavior problems in children. *Journal of Marriage and Family, 48*, 295–307.

Reid, M., Landesman, S., Treder, R., & Jaccard, J. (1989). 'My family and friends': Six- to twelve-year-old children's perceptions of social support. *Child Development, 60*(4), 896–910.

Rogers, M. J., & Holmbeck, G. N. (1997). Effects of interparental aggression on children's adjustment: The moderating role of cognitive appraisal and coping. *Journal of Family Psychology, 11*, 125–130.

Sameroff, A. (2010). A unified theory of development: A dialectic integration of nature and nurture. *Child Development, 81*(1), 6–22.

Schaefer, E. S. (1965). Children's report of parental behavior: An inventory. *Child Development, 36*, 413–424.

Schenck, C. E., Braver, S. L., Wolchik, S. A., Saenz, D., Cookston, J. T., & Fabricius, W. V. (2009). Relations between mattering to step- and non-residential fathers and adolescent mental health. *Fathering, 7*(1), 70–90.

Schofield, T., Castenada, E., Parke, R. D., & Coltrane, S. (2008). Eye contact in Mexican American and European American parent–child dyads. *Journal of Nonverbal Behavior, 17*, 171–186.

Stattin, H., & Kerr, M. (2000). Parental monitoring: A reinterpretation. *Child Development, 71*(4), 1072–1085.

Steinberg, L. (2010). A behavioral scientist looks at the science of adolescent brain development. *Brain and Cognition, 72*(1), 160–164.

Stright, A., & Bales, S. (2003). Coparenting quality: Contributions of child and parent characteristics. *Family Relations, 52*(3), 232–240.

Thayer, S., Updegraff, K., & Delgado, M. (2008). Conflict resolution in Mexican American adolescents' friendships: Links with culture, gender and friendship quality. *Journal of Youth and Adolescence, 37*(7), 783–797. doi:10.1007/s10964-007-9253-8.

Updegraff, K. A., Umaña-Taylor, A. J., Perez-Brena, N., & Pflieger, J. (2012). Mother–daughter conflict and adjustment in Mexican-origin families: Exploring the role of family and sociocultural context. In L. P. Juang & A. J. Umaña-Taylor (Eds.), *Family conflict among Chinese- and Mexican-origin adolescents and their parents in the U.S. New Directions for Child and Adolescent Development, 135*, 59–81.

Wadsworth, M. E., Raviv, T., Compas, B. E., & Connor-Smith, J. K. (2005). Parent and adolescent responses to poverty-related stress: Tests of mediated and moderated coping models. *Journal of Child and Family Studies, 14*, 283–298.

Windle, M., Miller-Tutzauer, C., Barnes, G. M., & Welte, J. (1991). Adolescent perceptions of help-seeking resources for substance abuse. *Child Development, 62*(1), 179–189.

Youniss, J., & Smollar, J. (1985). *Adolescent relations with mothers, fathers, and friends.* Chicago: University of Chicago Press.

JEFFREY T. COOKSTON *is an associate professor of psychology at San Francisco State University. E-mail: cookston@sfsu.edu, webpage: http://bss.sfsu.edu/devpsych/jcookston/*

ANDRES F. OLIDE *is a graduate student in the Graduate School of Education at University of California, Riverside. E-mail: andres.olide@email.ucr.edu*

MICHELE A. ADAMS *is an associate professor of sociology at Tulane University. E-mail: madams2@tulane.edu*

WILLIAM V. FABRICIUS *is an associate professor of psychology at Arizona State University, Tempe. E-mail: William.Fabricius@asu.edu, webpage: http://psychology.clas.asu.edu/Fabricius*

ROSS D. PARKE *is a Distinguished Professor Emeritus of Psychology at the University of California, Riverside. E-mail: ross.parke@ucr.edu*

Fuligni, A. J. (2012). Gaps, conflicts, and arguments between adolescents and their parents. In L. P. Juang & A. J. Umaña-Taylor (Eds.), *Family conflict among Chinese- and Mexican-origin adolescents and their parents in the U.S. New Directions for Child and Adolescent Development, 135*, 105–110.

6

Gaps, Conflicts, and Arguments Between Adolescents and Their Parents

Andrew J. Fuligni

Abstract

Parent–adolescent conflict appears to be similar across different immigrant generations and cultural groups in frequency and implications for adjustment. However, the same level of argumentation may mask hidden conflictual feelings that are not expressed. Why an acculturation gap leads to such conflictual feelings in some adolescents and not others is still not well understood. Addressing this and other important issues of parent–adolescent difference by clearly separating acculturation gaps, conflictual feelings, and actual arguments would go a long way toward helping us to understand the role of family relationships in the adaptation and adjustment of adolescents from Asian and Latin American backgrounds. © 2012 Wiley Periodicals, Inc.

Developmentalists have long been fascinated by the differences between children and their parents during adolescence. G. Stanley Hall and Freud believed family conflict to be inevitable during the teenage years, arguing that it was a necessary part of the process by which children separate from their parents (Freud, 1969; Hall, 1904). Concern over the "generation gap" emerged during the turbulent 1960s and 1970s and commentators often believed that teenagers and their parents lived in distinct cultural worlds with frequently colliding world views (Coleman, 1961). As with many ideas that emphasized the inevitable turmoil of adolescence, these views did not hold up very well in the face of systematic research on normative populations of adolescents. Numerous studies showed actual conflict between parents and teenagers to be relatively infrequent squabbles over the mundane details of everyday life, and that family members generally shared the same views over fundamental issues such as morality, religion, and politics (Douvan & Adelson, 1966; Steinberg, 1990). Rather than evidence of estrangement, the minor differences and occasional arguments that occur during adolescence are seen as evidence of a gradual realignment of parent–child relationships to accommodate the increasingly mature and competent adolescent (Smetana, 2008).

Scholars of immigrant families have a similar fascination with the differences between children and their parents, with good reason. Juang and Umaña-Taylor (this volume) nicely highlight in their introduction how immigrant families experience both developmental and cultural sources of conflict during the teenage years. In addition to the differences that normatively emerge as children enter adolescence, potential sources of conflict arise from the fact that teenagers from immigrant families generally acculturate to the host society more quickly than parents. Adolescents from immigrant families have greater exposure to the dominant norms and values of the host society as a result from attending school and greater facility with the language of the host country. These norms and values often diverge from those of the parents' native culture, particularly in areas such as independence, autonomy, and romantic relationships. Therefore, discussions of immigrant families have emphasized the inevitability of such "acculturation gaps" and "acculturation conflicts" and the challenges they present to families and the adjustment of their children (e.g., Kwak, 2003).

Interestingly, similar to earlier work on adolescents more broadly, systematic research on normative samples of immigrant families have brought into question the inevitability of conflict and the risks of adolescents being more acculturated to the host society than their parents. As Juang and Umaña-Taylor (this volume) describe, studies have often found no generational differences in the frequency of conflict between adolescents and their parents and a recent review suggested few signs of maladjustment among teenagers who are more acculturated than their parents (Chung, Flook, & Fuligni, 2009; Fuligni, 1998; Telzer, 2010).

The problem is that many scholars and the families themselves have difficulty reconciling such findings with what they know and experience in their everyday lives. As a member of an immigrant family once told me when hearing about the research summarized here, "I can see the results, but I just can't believe that they are true. They do not describe my experience or that of my friends." This is a common refrain among members of immigrant families and it echoes similar reactions from families more generally when they are told about research suggesting that adolescence is generally not a time of heightened family conflict. Children and their parents, whether immigrant or not, see adolescence as a challenging time because they *know* and *feel* the differences between themselves, differences that either did not exist or were not evident before.

One way to reconcile these reactions with the actual research is to distinguish between acculturation gaps, feelings of conflict, and actual arguments between adolescents and their parents. Distinguishing between these three types of parent–adolescent difference also provides a way to understand the findings presented in the chapters in this volume.

Acculturation gaps generally refer to differences in cultural-related values, norms, and behaviors between adolescents and their parents. Gaps are estimated by independently assessing these constructs among different family members and computing difference scores. In general, the normative pattern is that adolescents in immigrant families tend to score higher on attitudes and behaviors that reflect an orientation toward the host culture (e.g., American society) and parents tend to score higher on those that reflect an orientation toward parents' culture of origin (e.g., Mexican society). When measured in such a manner, these normative acculturation gaps do not appear to be problematic for adolescent adjustment (Telzer, 2010). That is, simply having a greater orientation toward the host society than parents generally does not comprise adolescents' psychological and behavioral well-being.

Having conflictual feelings about such acculturation gaps, however, is another story. In their chapter, Juang and colleagues (Juang, Syed, Cookston, Wang, & Kim, this volume) present results from two independent studies showing that scores on Lee, Choe, Kim, and Ngo's (2000) Asian American Family Conflicts Scale have associations with psychological adjustment that are independent of everyday conflict arguments, and that these associations are mediated by parenting and family cohesion. It is important to note that the Lee scale does not assess actual arguments or simple acculturation gaps. Rather, it assesses conflictual feelings about acculturation gaps with items such as "Your parents want you to sacrifice personal interests for the sake of the family, but you feel this is unfair" and "Your parents always compare you to others, but you want them to accept you for being yourself." As such, it taps the type of internal conflict that many children from immigrant parents feel without necessarily expressing this in an actual argument with parents. In that sense, it is assessing the same conflictual feelings that Qin et al. (this volume) observed in their qualitative interviews with Chinese immigrant families. Both parents and adolescents sense this difference between them and find it threatening, which is likely why family cohesion showed up as a mediator in the Juang and colleagues chapter. These conflictual feelings not only threaten the dyadic relationship, but they also potentially threaten family cohesion as a whole because they question the unity of the family around shared values and norms.

Yet these conflictual feelings are not necessarily expressed in open conflict, which may be why prior studies have observed few generational and ethnic differences in everyday arguments and conflicts between adolescents and their parents. Qin and colleagues (Qin, Chang, Han, & Chee, this volume) attribute the lack of open argumentation to a "vertical ingroup conflict resolution style" by which adolescents are more hesitant to openly question and challenge their parents. It is possible that this conflict resolution style is the reason why few generational and ethnic differences in actual conflict are observed in several studies. Based upon the conflictual feelings adolescents have about their acculturation gaps, those from immigrant families might be expected to have greater everyday conflict than other teenagers. A reticence to openly challenge parents may act to suppress that potential generational difference.

Considering these three aspects of parent–adolescent difference (i.e., acculturation gap, conflictual feelings, actual arguments) also allows for the type of analysis conducted by Updegraff and colleagues (Updegraff, Umaña-Taylor, Perez-Brena, & Pflieger, this volume). They report an interesting pattern by which the association between conflict and adjustment is stronger among adolescents in families that demonstrate a nonnormative acculturation gap in which the parents were more oriented toward Anglo culture and less oriented toward Mexican culture than their teenagers. Interestingly, Telzer's (2010) review of acculturation gap research suggests that this type of gap is more likely to show patterns of maladjustment than other types of gaps. The reasons for this are unclear, but one is tempted to speculate that the conflictual feelings and threats to family cohesion in these families are greater than those showing other types of acculturation gaps. Future work, including the type of in-depth qualitative interviews conducted by Qin et al. (this volume), would aid in understanding this intriguing pattern.

Collectively, the papers in this volume help to describe what is similar and what is different about family relationships among adolescents from different ethnic and immigrant backgrounds. Frequency of open argumentation and conflict appear to be quite similar across groups in both frequency and their implications for adjustment. Cookston and colleagues (Cookston, Olide, Adams, Fabricius, & Parke, this volume) also show how support seeking after instances of actual parent–adolescent conflict is similar between those from Latino and European American backgrounds.

However, the same level of actual conflict among different generations and culture groups may mask hidden conflictual feelings that are not expressed because of different cultural traditions regarding the appropriateness of open argumentation between children and their parents. Why an acculturation gap leads to such conflictual feelings in some adolescents and not others is still not well understood and is an important direction for future research. Addressing this and other important issues of parent–adolescent difference by clearly separating acculturation gaps, conflictual feelings, and actual arguments would go a long way toward helping us to understand the role of family relationships in the adaptation and adjustment of adolescents from Asian and Latin American backgrounds.

References

Chung, G., Flook, L., & Fuligni, A. J. (2009). Daily family conflict and emotional distress among adolescents from Latin American, Asian, and European backgrounds. *Developmental Psychology, 45*, 1406–1415.

Coleman, J. (1961). *The adolescent society*. Glencoe, IL: Free Press.

Cookston, J. T., Olide, A. F., Adams, M., Fabricius, W. V., Parke, R. D. (2012). Guided cognitive reframing of adolescent–father conflict: Who Mexican American and European American adolescents seek and why. In L. P. Juang & A. J. Umaña-Taylor (Eds.), *Family conflict among Chinese- and Mexican-origin adolescents and their parents in the U.S. New Directions for Child and Adolescent Development, 135*, 83–103.

Douvan, E., & Adelson, J. (1966). *The adolescent experience*. New York, NY: Wiley.

Freud, A. (1969). Adolescence as a developmental disturbance. In G. Caplan & S. Ledovici (Eds.), *Adolescence: Psychosocial perspectives* (pp. 5–10). Cambridge, MA: Harvard University Press.

Fuligni, A. J. (1998). Authority, autonomy, and parent–adolescent conflict and cohesion: A study of adolescents from Mexican, Chinese, Filipino, and European backgrounds. *Developmental Psychology, 34*, 782–792.

Hall, G. S. (1904). *Adolescence: Its psychology and its relations to physiology, anthropology, sociology, sexuality, crime, religion and education*. New York, NY: D. Appleton & Co.

Juang, L. P., Syed, M., Cookston, J. T., Wang, Y., & Kim, S. Y. (2012). Acculturation-based and everyday family conflict in Chinese American Families. In L. P. Juang & A. J. Umaña-Taylor (Eds.), *Family conflict among Chinese- and Mexican-origin adolescents and their parents in the U.S. New Directions for Child and Adolescent Development, 135*, 13–34.

Juang, L. P., & Umaña-Taylor, A. J. (2012). Family conflict among Chinese- and Mexican-origin adolescents and their parents in the U.S.: An introduction. In L. P. Juang & A. J. Umaña-Taylor (Eds.), *Family conflict among Chinese- and Mexican-origin adolescents and their parents in the U.S. New Directions for Child and Adolescent Development, 135*, 1–11.

Kwak, K. (2003). Adolescents and their parents: A review of intergenerational family relations for immigrant and non-immigrant families. *Human Development, 46*(2–3), 115–136. doi:10.1159/000068581

Lee, R. M., Choe, J., Kim, G., & Ngo, V. (2000). Construction of the Asian American family conflicts scale. *Journal of Counseling Psychology, 47*(2), 211–222.

Qin, D. B., Chang, T-F., Han E-J., & Chee, G. (2012). Conflicts and communication between high-achieving Chinese American adolescents and their parents. In L. P. Juang & A. J. Umaña-Taylor (Eds.), *Family Conflict among Chinese- and*

Mexican-Origin Adolescents and Their Parents in the U.S. *New Directions for Child and Adolescent Development, 135,* 35–57.

Smetana, J. G. (2008). Conflicting views of conflict. *Monographs of the Society for Research in Child Development, 73,* 161–168.

Steinberg, L. (1990). Autonomy, conflict, and harmony in the family relationship. In S. S. Feldman & G. Elliot (Eds.), *At the threshold: The developing adolescent* (pp. 255–276). Cambridge, MA: Harvard University Press.

Telzer, E. H. (2010). Expanding the acculturation gap-distress model: An integrative review of research. *Human Development, 53,* 313–340.

Updegraff, K. A., Umaña-Taylor, A. J., Perez-Brena, N., & Pflieger, J. (2012). Mother–daughter conflict and adjustment in Mexican-origin families: Exploring the role of family and sociocultural context. In L. P. Juang & A. J. Umaña-Taylor (Eds.), *Family conflict among Chinese- and Mexican-origin adolescents and their parents in the U.S. New Directions for Child and Adolescent Development, 135,* 59–81.

ANDREW J. FULIGNI *is a professor of psychiatry and psychology at the University of California at Los Angeles. E-mail: afuligni@ucla.edu, webpage: http://www.semel.ucla.edu/aei*

INDEX

Abelmann, N., 29
Acculturation gaps: defined, 4, 107; inevitability of, 106
Acculturation-based conflict and everyday conflict, 13, 16–30
Active-approach coping, 84, 85
Adams, M., 83, 103
Adaptive culture, defined, 8
Adelson, J., 106
Adolescent motherhood, overview of, 61–62. *See also* Mother–daughter conflict in Mexican-origin families, 59–78
Aiken, L. S., 69, 90
Alfaro, E. C., 63
Arnold, B., 65
Asian American Family Conflict Scale, 22, 26, 107

Baker, H., 87
Bales, S., 95
Barber, B., 65
Barber, J. G., 84
Barnes, G. M., 87
Barr, A., 84
Barrera, M., 84
Beam, M., 86
Behavior Problem Inventory, 90
Berry, J. W., 75, 76
Birman, D., 60, 62, 63, 76
Blakemore, S.-J., 29
Borkowski, J. G., 61
Bradley, J., 84
Bronfenbrenner, U., 14, 30, 60, 62
Brown, B., 87
Bruner, J., 2, 28
Buchanan, C. M., 87
Buhrmester, D., 86
Bush, K., 86

Campione-Barr, N., 2
Castenada, E., 87
Cauce, A. M., 20, 61, 62
Chang, T.-F., 6, 27, 35, 57, 108
Chao, R. K., 36, 37
Charman, T., 29
Chee, G., 6, 27, 35, 57, 108
Chen, C., 5, 8, 18, 20, 36, 86

Cheung, B. Y., 17
Chinese-American adolescents, conflicts between parents and high-achieving, 35–54
Chinese-American families, two types of conflict in, 13–30
Chiu, C. Y., 36
Choe, J., 17, 36
Choudhury, S., 29
Chu, J. Y., 39
Chua, A., 36, 48
Chua, S., 36
Chudek, M., 17
Chung, G., 5, 84, 106
Clingempeel, W., 87
Coffelt, T. A., 98
Cohen, J., 68, 90
Cohen, P., 90
Coleman, J., 106
Coleman, M., 87
Collectivism, defined, 15
Collins, W. A., 2, 16, 60
Coltrane, S., 87, 99
Compas, B. E., 84
Comstock, J., 40, 54
Conflict: constructive versus destructive, 28; everyday and acculturation-based, 13, 16–30
Conflict resolution styles, 40–41, 51–52
Confucian values, 36, 37
Conger, R. D., 61
Connor-Smith, J. K., 84
Contreras, J. M., 62, 73, 74
Cookston, J., 5, 6, 7, 13, 19, 28, 36, 74, 83, 84, 86, 99, 103, 107, 108
Coon, H. M., 15
Cooper, C. R., 37, 39, 87
Corbin, J., 42
Costigan, C. L., 17, 20, 27, 36, 39
Coy, K. C., 2, 16
Crane, D. R., 36
Crockett, L. J., 39
Crouter, A. C., 60, 61, 62, 63
Cuellar, I., 65

Daddis, C., 2
Davies, L. C., 87
Deardorff, J., 84

111

DeCarlo Santiago, C., 84
Delfabbro, P., 84
Delgado, M. Y., 5, 60, 64, 88
Depression Inventory, Children's, 42
Depression Scale, Center for Epidemiological Studies, 65
Derogatis, L. R., 90
Dishion, T. J., 84
Dokis, D. P., 17, 27, 36, 39
Domenech-Rodríguez, M., 61, 62
Dong, Q., 18, 86
Dornbusch, S. M., 87
Douvan, E., 106
Dumka, L. E., 89
Dunn, J., 87

Eccles, J. S., 60, 62, 65, 76, 77
Ecological systems model, Bronfenbrenner's, 14
Educational pressure, conflicts related to, 43–46
Erikson, E. H., 61
Etchison, K., 20
Everyday conflict and acculturation-based conflict, 13, 16–30

Fabricius, W. V., 5, 83, 103, 108
Failures in school, reactions to, 44–45
Family obligation and harmony, emphasis on, 5–6
Farrugia, S., 86
Father-adolescent conflict, guided cognitive reframing of, 83–100
Feldman, S. S., 2
Fincham, F. D., 89
Fine, M. A., 62, 76
Flook, L., 5, 84, 106
Formoso, D., 84
Freeman, H., 87
Freud, A.., 106
Fujimoto, K., 4, 39
Fujita, K., 36, 39
Fuligni, A. J., 2, 5, 7, 8, 17, 18, 61, 73, 84, 105, 106, 110
Furman, W., 86
Future research, 8–9

Gaines, C., 61, 73
Ganong, L. H., 87
García Coll, C., 3, 8, 9, 60
Gonzales, N., 62, 70, 84
Goodnow, J. J., 14
Granic, I., 84
Greenberger, E., 8, 18, 86

Grych, J. H., 89
Guided cognitive reframing, overview of, 84–86
Guo, M.-S., 18, 86

Hafen Jr., M., 36
Hall, G. S., 106
Hamm, J. V., 36
Han, E.-J., 6, 27, 35, 57, 108
Harris, V. S., 64
Hayes, A. F., 23
Heine, S. J., 17
Hepp, B., 84
Hesselbrock, V., 84
Hetherington, E., 87
Hill, J. P., 61
Ho, D.Y.F., 36, 37, 38
Hofstede, G., 15, 87
Hollenstein, T., 84
Holmbeck, G. N., 84
Hopkins Symptom Checklist, 90
Huang, X., 5
Hubbard, E., 100
Hwang, K. K., 37, 38, 39, 40, 51, 53
Hwang, W.-C., 4

Ikhlas, M., 62
Individualism–collectivism (IC), defined, 15–16
Intergenerational Conflict Inventory, 22

Jaccard, J., 86
Jose, P. E., 28
Juang, L., 1, 5, 6, 11, 13, 17, 19, 34, 36, 38, 39, 40, 43, 84, 99, 106, 107, 108
Juntos Project, overview of, 64
Jutengren, G., 40, 54

Kağitçibaşi, C., 15
Kang, H., 29
Kao, E. M.-C., 39
Keefe, S. E., 87
Kemmelmeier, M., 15
Keogh, D., 61
Kerr, M., 89, 95
Killoren, S., 88
Kim, G., 17, 36, 84, 107
Kim, S. Y., 5, 13, 20, 34, 36, 107
Kim-Prieto, C., 29
Kitayama, S., 15, 40
Knight, G. P., 64, 70, 90
Kovacs, M., 42
Krane, S., 41
Kupanoff, K., 61

Kurtines, W., 62, 76, 77
Kwak, K., 4, 16, 17, 18, 37, 39, 41

Lam, C. M., 37
Lam, M., 8
Landesman, S., 86
Language barriers, conflicts related to, 47–48
Larson, J. H., 36
Lau, A. S., 9, 17, 60, 61, 73, 75
Laursen, B., 2, 9, 16, 17, 18, 20, 60, 61, 73
Lazarus, R. S., 84, 85
Lee, R. M., 17, 20, 21, 26, 27, 36, 39, 40, 41
Lee, S.-H., 39
Leidy, M., 89
Leite, R. W., 88
Leong, F. T. L., 39
Lerner, J. V., 60, 62, 76
Lerner, R. M., 60, 62, 76
Lester, J., 18, 86
Li, J., 5
Liang, J., 17
Lim, S.-L., 17
Lin, P.-Y., 36, 39
Lockwood, C. M., 23
Loneliness Questionnaire, Revised UCLA, 22
Louie, V., 37, 48
Lynch, M. E., 61

Maccoby, E. E., 87
MacKinnon, D. P., 23
Madden, T., 3
Magnuson, K., 9
Maldonado, R., 65
Manke, B. A., 61
Marcia, J., 61
Marín, B. V., 62
Marín, G., 62
Markus, H, 15, 40, 61
Matsumoto, D., 15
Maxwell, J., 42
McCabe, K., 17
McHale, S. M., 61, 63, 64
McKenry, P. C., 88
McLean, , 29
McLoyd, V. C., 3, 73
Mexican American Cultural Values Scale, 90
Mexican-origin families, mother–daughter conflict in, 59–78
Miller-Tutzauer, C., 87

Montemayor, R., 40
Moon, U. J., 5
Morgan-Lopez, A. A., 70
Morris, A. S., 2, 5, 16, 17, 18
Mother–daughter conflict in Mexican-origin families, 59–78
Muthén, B., 21, 94
Muthén, L. K., 21, 94

Nagi, S. W., 36
Narang, D., 62
Narayanan, P., 28
Ngo, V., 17, 36, 107
Nomaguchi, K., 84, 86, 87
Nsamenang, A. B., 15

O'Connor, T. G., 87
Offer, D., 17
Ohannessian, C., 84
Okazaki, S., 15, 29, 48
Okubo, Y., 39, 41, 53
Olide, A. F., 5, 83, 103, 108
Ong, A., 3, 17
Oyserman, D., 15

Padilla, A. M., 87
Pakaliniskiene, V., 95
Palmerus, K., 40, 54
Parent Behavior Inventory, Children's Report of, 89
Parenting Practices Questionnaire, 22
Parke, R. D., 5, 83, 87, 99, 103, 108
Pasch, L. A., 5, 60, 61, 73, 75
Passel, J. S., 3, 4
Perez-Brena, N., 5, 27, 59, 81, 99, 108
Person-environment mismatch, 62, 76
Peterson, J. L., 90
Pflieger, J., 5, 27, 59, 81, 108
Phinney, J. S., 3, 17
Polichar, D., 87
Portes, A., 2, 4, 16, 17, 18, 26, 76, 77
Preacher, K. J., 23

Qin, D. B., 5, 6, 8, 17, 20, 26, 27, 28, 35, 37, 39, 40, 41, 46, 57, 108

Racist remarks and attitudes, 46–47
Radloff, L., 65
Raviv, T., 84
Reid, M., 86
Respect for elders, 26
Reynolds, C. R., 42
Richmond, B. O., 42
Rivera, F. I., 2, 17

Rogers, M. J., 84
Roosa, M. W., 64, 89
Rosenberg, M., 42
Rosenberg Self-Esteem scale, 22
Rosenthal, D. A., 2
Ruddy, K., 84
Rumbaut, R., 2, 4, 16, 17, 18, 26, 76, 77
Russell, S. T., 39, 53

Saenz, D., 70
Saltzman, 84
Sameroff, A., 87
Saw, A., 15
Scaramella, L. V., 61
Schaefer, E. S. 89
Schenck, C. E., 89
Schofield, T. J., 87, 88
Schrodt, P., 40
Schwartz, S. J., 5
Seid, M., 89
Shanshan, L., 29
Shea, J. M-Y., 36, 39
Sinatra, F., 50
Sirolli, A., 70
Smetana, J., 2, 5, 8, 15, 17, 18, 25, 26, 28, 30, 61, 64, 73, 106
Smollar, J., 2, 86
Social domain theory, 25
Stattin, H., 89, 95
Steinberg, L., 2, 5, 16, 17, 18, 99, 106
Strauss, A., 42
Stress, coping with, 86
Stright, A., 95
Stuart, J., 28
Sturgess, W., 87
Su, J., 36
Suarez-Orozco, C., 8, 54
Suárez-Orozco, M., 54
Sue, S., 48
Sung, B., 39
Syed, M., 5, 13, 17, 19, 34, 36, 40, 84, 107
Szapocznik, J., 62, 76, 77

Takagi, M., 5, 17, 40
Tamis-LeMonda, C. S., 5, 15, 16, 28, 29, 30, 53
Tan, C. B., 38
Teichman, J., 62

Telzer, E. H., 4, 106, 107, 108
Thayer, S. M., 63, 64, 88
Thomsen, 84
Thorne, 29
Tiger mothers/fathers, 48–49
Todorova, I., 54
Treder, R., 86
Triandis, H. C., 15
Tseng, V., 8, 37
Tu, W. M., 36, 37
Turiel, E., 25

Uba, L., 38, 39
Umaña-Taylor, A. J., 1, 5, 11, 27, 59, 62, 63, 64, 76, 81, 106, 108
Updegraff, K. A., 5, 6, 27, 59, 60, 61, 63, 64, 73, 75, 76, 81, 84, 88, 108

Vega, E., 99

Wadsworth, M. E., 84
Wang, Y., 5, 13, 34, 36, 84, 107
Waninger, K., 84
Ward, C., 28
Way, N., 36
Weaver, S. R., 20
Weed, K., 61
Well-being, family conflict and pathways to, 19–26
Welsh, M., 87
Welte, J., 87
West, S. G., 69, 90
Wheeler, L. A., 5, 60
Whiteman, S. D., 63, 64
Whitman, T. L., 61
Williams, J., 23
Windle, M., 87, 97
Wood, J. J., 4, 39
Wu, C., 36
Wurf, E., 61

Yang, K. S., 37
Yau, J., 5, 18, 26
Yeh, C. J., 36, 39
Yeh, M., 17
Yoshida, E., 36
Youniss, J., 2, 86

Zill, N., 90

NEW DIRECTIONS FOR CHILD AND ADOLESCENT DEVELOPMENT
ORDER FORM SUBSCRIPTION AND SINGLE ISSUES

DISCOUNTED BACK ISSUES:

Use this form to receive 20% off all back issues of *New Directions for Child and Adolescent Development*. All single issues priced at **$23.20** (normally $29.00)

TITLE	ISSUE NO.	ISBN

Call 888-378-2537 or see mailing instructions below. When calling, mention the promotional code JBNND to receive your discount. For a complete list of issues, please visit www.josseybass.com/go/ndcad

SUBSCRIPTIONS: (1 YEAR, 4 ISSUES)

☐ New Order ☐ Renewal

U.S.	☐ Individual: $89	☐ Institutional: $315
CANADA/MEXICO	☐ Individual: $89	☐ Institutional: $355
ALL OTHERS	☐ Individual: $113	☐ Institutional: $389

Call 888-378-2537 or see mailing and pricing instructions below.
Online subscriptions are available at www.onlinelibrary.wiley.com

ORDER TOTALS:

Issue / Subscription Amount: $ _____
Shipping Amount: $ _____
(for single issues only – subscription prices include shipping)
Total Amount: $ _____

SHIPPING CHARGES:
First Item $6.00
Each Add'l Item $2.00

(No sales tax for U.S. subscriptions. Canadian residents, add GST for subscription orders. Individual rate subscriptions must be paid by personal check or credit card. Individual rate subscriptions may not be resold as library copies.)

BILLING & SHIPPING INFORMATION:

☐ **PAYMENT ENCLOSED:** *(U.S. check or money order only. All payments must be in U.S. dollars.)*
☐ **CREDIT CARD:** ☐ VISA ☐ MC ☐ AMEX

Card number _____ Exp. Date _____
Card Holder Name _____ Card Issue # _____
Signature _____ Day Phone _____

☐ **BILL ME:** *(U.S. institutional orders only. Purchase order required.)*

Purchase order # _____
Federal Tax ID 13559302 • GST 89102-8052

Name _____
Address _____
Phone _____ E-mail _____

Copy or detach page and send to: **John Wiley & Sons, One Montgomery Street, Suite 1200, San Francisco, CA 94104-4594**

Order Form can also be faxed to: **888-481-2665**

PROMO JBNND